Angela Creese

Revising Cookery

BELL & HYMAN · LONDON

Published as *Revision Notes for O level and CSE Cookery* in 1981 by
Bell & Hyman Limited, Denmark House, 37–39 Queen Elizabeth Street, London SE1 2QB

First published in 1969 by Allman & Son Ltd

Reprinted 1971
Second (metric) edition 1973
Reprinted 1974, 1976, 1978
Third edition 1981
Reprinted 1983

Fourth edition under the title **Revising Cookery**, 1983

British Library Cataloguing in Publication Data

Creese, Angela
  Revising Cookery.
  1. Cookery — Problems, exercises, etc.
  I. Title
  641.5'076   TX652.7

  ISBN 0 7135 1385 3

Typeset by Inforum Ltd, Portsmouth
Printed in Great Britain by
Richard Clay (the Chaucer Press) Ltd
Bungay, Suffolk

Contents

Proteins

Body uses

1. GROWTH and REPAIR of body.
2. Any extra the body uses for heat and energy.

Composition

Carbon, Hydrogen, Oxygen and Nitrogen (main elements).

Notes

1. Proteins may be divided into two classes:
   (*a*) Animal proteins
   (*b*) Vegetable proteins.
2. All proteins are made up of AMINO ACIDS.
3. There are at least twenty-two different amino acids in proteins.
4. The body can change some amino acids into others.
5. ESSENTIAL AMINO ACIDS are essential for growth and repair.
   There are ten of these.
   The body cannot manufacture them.
   The body must get them from food.
6. Animal proteins generally contain all the essential amino acids ('Biologically complete').
   Vegetable proteins generally lack one or more essential amino acids ('Biologically incomplete').
   But:　　(*a*) Gelatine is an animal protein but lacks four essential amino acids.
   　　　　(*b*) Soya bean flour is a vegetable protein but contains the essential amino acids.
7. The body needs both animal and vegetable proteins.
8. Texturized vegetable protein (TVP) resembles meat and costs less. Proteins of plants, e.g. soya beans, are fortified with the most important minerals and vitamins which meat contains such as iron, thiamin, riboflavin and vitamin B_{12}.

Advantages of TVP

1. It is cheaper than meat.
2. Can be made into a variety of foods, e.g. sausages, pies, curries, stews, hamburgers etc.
3. Easily stored; does not need to be refrigerated.
4. Absorbs fat and water well when cooked.

5. Contains very little fat and no gristle and there is therefore less waste.
6. Can be used with fresh meat to make it go further.
7. Very useful to increase protein content of the diet.
8. The nutritional value of TVP compares well with fresh meat.
9. Very useful for enabling vegetarians to obtain sufficient protein.

Sources

Animal: Meat, milk, eggs, fish, cheese.
Vegetable: Cereals, pulses, nuts.

Effects of heat

1. Coagulates ('sets').
2. Overheating
   (a) makes protein shrink and become hard,
   (b) makes it indigestible.

Digestion

1. Partly broken up in stomach.
2. Change to amino acids completed in small intestine.
3. Absorbed through walls of small intestine.
4. Carried by blood to liver, then into general circulation.
5. Used for growth and repair, or energy.
6. The body cannot store protein.
7. Carbohydrate food should be eaten with protein food so that the protein can be used for body building.

Fat

Body uses

1. Energy for WORK and WARMTH.
2. To form BODY FAT.

   Also: (a) Fat can be stored as a reserve source of heat and energy.
   (b) Fat protects vital organs, e.g. kidneys.
   (c) Fat is a more concentrated energy food than carbohydrates.

Composition

1. Carbon, Hydrogen, Oxygen.
2. All fats are made up of FATTY ACIDS and GLYCEROL.

3. The fatty acids give fats:
    (a) Their particular flavour.
    (b) Their hardness or softness, e.g. lard is soft, beef fat is hard, oils are liquid at normal temperature.
4. Fatty acids can be 'saturated' or 'unsaturated'.
    (a) Saturated fatty acids, e.g. palmitic acid and stearic acid in hard fats (lard, suet, cocoa butter); butyric acid in milk fat and butter.
    (b) Unsaturated fatty acids are of two kinds — Monounsaturated and Polyunsaturated.
    Oleic acid (Monounsaturated) in all fats, especially olive oil.
    Linoleic acid in vegetable seed oils, e.g. corn (maize) oil and soya bean oil. Also small amounts in pork.
    Arachidonic acid — small amounts in some animal fats.
    (c) Linoleic, linolenic and arachidonic acids are called 'essential fatty acids'. The body needs them but can't make them.
    (d) Polyunsaturated fatty acids help prevent build up of cholesterol in blood and are therefore regarded as helpful in the prevention of heart disease.

Kinds

Animal fats.
Vegetable fats.

Sources

Animal: Butter, cream, cheese, egg yolk.
             Meat fat, dripping, lard, suet.
             Oily fish, fish liver oils.
Vegetable: Olive oil, nut and seed oils.

Note: Margarine may be made of all vegetable fat or a mixture of vegetable and animal fat.

Effects of heat

1. It melts.
2. Any moisture evaporates.
3. Overheating causes most fat to decompose into fatty acids and glycerol. This makes it indigestible.

Digestion

1. Emulsified in the small intestine.
2. Absorbed through walls of the small intestine.

3. Some used at once for energy.
4. The rest is stored.

Also:　　　(*a*) Fats take longer to digest than other foods.
　　　　　(*b*) Fats should always be eaten with carbohydrate foods,
　　　　　　　　otherwise the fat will be incompletely burnt and cause
　　　　　　　　KETOSIS (sickness).

Carbohydrates

Body uses

1. Energy for WORK and WARMTH.
2. A little stored as GLYCOGEN in the liver.
3. Extra is converted into FAT in the body.

Composition

Carbon, Hydrogen, Oxygen.

Kinds

Sugars may be simple or compound.
　Simple: Monosaccharides (Glucose, Fructose, Galactose)
　Double: Disaccharides (Sucrose, Maltose, Lactose)
Starch — Polysaccharide — composed of large numbers of glucose units.
Cellulose — Polysaccharide — composed of large numbers of glucose
　units (also called 'dietary fibre').
Pectin and Dextrin are both complex polysaccharides.

Sources

Sugars:　　　Cane and beet sugar, honey, jam.
　　　　　　Syrup, fresh and dried fruit, some vegetables, e.g. beetroot.
Starch:　　　Cereals, e.g. wheat, oats, barley.
　　　　　　Food made with cereals, e.g. cakes and puddings.
　　　　　　Potatoes and pulses.
Cellulose:　　Framework of vegetables and fruits.
　　　　　　Cannot be digested by human beings but useful as roughage.

Pectin

A complicated carbohydrate, present in just ripe fruit, sets jam. No food
value.

Cooking apples, citrus fruits, gooseberries, blackcurrents, plums are rich in pectin.

Strawberries, blackberries, pears, poor.

Dextrin

A complicated carbohydrate.

Starch is partly changed into dextrin when cooked, e.g. crust of loaves, toast.

Easier to digest than starch.

Effects of heat

Sugar:
Dry heat — Sugar melts, the caramelises, then burns.
Wet heat — Sugar dissolves and becomes a syrup, caramelises and burns when water has evaporated.
Starch:
Dry heat — Changes into dextrin.
Wet heat — Starch grains soften, swell, burst.
Starch then dissolves in liquid and forms a paste.

Digestion

Sugar — complex sugars converted to glucose in the small intestine.
Glucose absorbed mainly through walls of small intestine.
Starch — partly broken down by saliva in mouth. Breakdown into glucose completed in small intestine.
The digested carbohydrates may be
(*a*) Used for energy at once.
(*b*) Stored as glycogen in liver and changed back to glucose when needed for energy.
(*c*) Stored as body fat.

Mineral elements

1. The name 'MINERALS' is given to elements which are found in the body apart from Carbon, Hydrogen, Oxygen and Nitrogen.
2. The minerals present in the largest amounts are CALCIUM and PHOSPHORUS.
3. Some other minerals necessary are Iron, Sodium, Potassium, Sulphur, Chlorine, Magnesium, Fluorine, Iodine, Copper and Manganese.

Body uses

1. As body building materials, e.g. for bones and teeth.
2. For making the cells of the body, e.g. muscles, nerves, liver, brain, etc.
3. For making body fluids, e.g. blood, digestive juices, sweat, etc.
4. For the normal working of the body, e.g. the clotting of blood during bleeding.

Calcium

1. Used for: (*a*) Making strong bones and teeth.
   (*b*) Keeping the muscles in good working order.
   (*c*) The clotting of blood.
2. Special (*a*) Children.
   needs (*b*) Expectant and nursing mothers.
   (*c*) Elderly people.
3. Too little: (*a*) Children don't grow properly. Get rickets and poor teeth.
   (*b*) Adults, bones brittle, teeth poor.
   (*c*) Blood won't clot properly.
4. Sources: (*a*) Milk and cheese (rich sources).
   (*b*) Bread (added to white flour), bones of sardines and salmon, hard water, eggs, green vegetables.

Phosphorus

1. Used for: (*a*) Making strong bones and teeth (combines with calcium).
   (*b*) Enables body to obtain energy from food.
   (*c*) Making cells of the body (especially of nerves and brain).
2. Sources: Found in most foods, especially milk, cheese, liver, kidney, meat, fish, eggs, bread.

Iron

1. Used for making the red colour in blood — HAEMOGLOBIN. Haemoglobin is needed to carry oxygen in the blood to the tissues so that fuel foods can be burnt to provide energy.
2. Special (*a*) Babies after the age of six months.
   needs: (*b*) Expectant and nursing mothers.
   (*c*) Girls and women when they are losing blood in monthly periods.
   Note: Iron is lost from the body
   (*a*) When bleeding occurs.
   (*b*) In the general wear and tear of the body.

3. Too little: (*a*) Get tired easily or faint.
              (*b*) May get anaemia.
4. Sources: (*a*) Liver, kidney, meat, corned beef, egg yolk.
            (*b*) Bread, dried fruit, black treacle, watercress (the iron in spinach cannot be used by the body).

Iodine

1. Used for the proper working of the THYROID gland. The thyroid gland controls mental and physical growth.
2. Special   (*a*) Expectant mothers.
  needs: (*b*) People living in parts of the country where there is too little iodine in the soil and water.
3. Too little: (*a*) Enlarged thyroid gland ('Goitre').
             (*b*) Babies deformed physically and mentally.
4. Sources: (*a*) Sea fish.   (*c*) Watercress, onions.
            (*b*) Iodised salt.   (*d*) Water.

Sodium

1. Used for all body fluids, to enable muscles to work properly.
2. Special   (*a*) In very hot weather.
  needs: (*b*) After strenuous exercise.
             (*c*) By people working in hot places.
  Note: Salt is lost from the body in perspiration and urine.
3. Too little: (*a*) Cramp of the muscles.
             (*b*) Headache, tiredness, sickness.
4. Sources: (*a*) Salt.
            (*b*) Bacon, cheese, kippers.

Fluorine

1. Used for forming healthy teeth and bones.
2. Sources: Some drinking water, fish.

Vitamins

Vitamin A (Axerophthol, Anti-infective vitamin).

1. Used for: (*a*) Growth of children.
          (*b*) Bones and teeth.
          (*c*) Healthy sight.
          (*d*) Healthy skin.

(e) Keeping linings of bronchial tubes, stomach, etc. moist.

(f) Helps resistance to disease.

Note: Body can store Vitamin A in the liver.

2. Found in: (a) As Vitamin A, in fatty parts of food. In fish liver oils, liver, kidney, egg yolk, butter, cheese, milk, margarine (added to).

   (b) As CAROTENE, body changes this into Vitamin A. Carrots, spinach, watercress, tomatoes, dried apricots.

3. Special needs: (a) Children.

   (b) Expectant and nursing mothers.

   (c) People who do not digest fat well may need fish liver oil capsules.

4. Too little: (a) Cannot see well in dim light. May become 'night blind' or completely blind.

   (b) Eyes, throat, etc. easily infected.

   (c) Skin rough and sore.

   (d) Bones and teeth do not form properly.

5. Effect of heat: Not affected by ordinary cooking.

6. In water — will not dissolve in water. Will dissolve in fat (called 'fat soluble').

Vitamin B group

There are at least eleven vitamins in this group. The body cannot store them so needs a daily supply. Three important ones are:

Vitamin B_1 (Thiamine)

Vitamin B_2 (Riboflavin)

Nicotinic Acid (Niacin)

Vitamin B_1 (Thiamin)

1. Used for: (a) Helping the body use carbohydrate for energy.

   (b) Growth and general health.

   (c) Strengthens nervous system.

2. Found in: (a) Yeast and yeast extracts.

   (b) Lean meat, pork, bacon, ham, liver.

   (c) Fish and fish roes, eggs.

   (d) Dried peas, beans, lentils, nuts, oatmeal.

   (e) Bread (added to most flour); whole grain cereals.

3. Special needs (a) People doing heavy work.

   (b) Children.

   (c) Expectant and nursing mothers.

4. Too little: (a) Growth of children slowed down.

(b) Loss of appetite, poor digestion.

(c) Feel tired, miserable, achey.

(d) Very little — may get disease called Beri-beri (not often found in England).

5. Effect of heat: (a) Not affected by ordinary cooking.

(b) More loss at very high temperature, e.g. pressure cooking, canning.

(c) Destroyed by bicarbonate of soda.

6. In water — will dissolve (water soluble).

Vitamin B₂ (Riboflavin)

1. Used for: (a) Helping body use food for energy.

(b) Helping body use food fats and amino acids.

(c) Helps growth.

2. Found in: (a) Yeast and yeast products.

(b) Lean meat, liver, kidney.

(c) Milk, cheese, eggs.

(d) Pulses, nuts, bread.

3. Special needs (a) Children.

(b) Expectant and nursing mothers.

4. Too little: (a) Growth of children slowed down.

(b) Cracks and sores at corners of mouth and sore tongue.

(c) Eyes may become misty.

5. Effect of heat: (a) Some lost in ordinary cooking.

(b) More lost at very high temperatures.

Some lost from milk left in sunlight.

6. In water — will dissolve (water soluble).

Nicotinic acid (Niacin)

1. Used for: (a) Helping the body use food for energy.

(b) Growth.

2. Found in: (a) Yeast and yeast products.

(b) Lean meat, liver, kidney.

(c) Herrings and white fish.

(d) Potatoes, whole grain cereals, bread.

3. Special needs: (a) Children.

(b) Expectant and nursing mothers.

4. Too little: (a) Growth in children slowed down.

(b) Skin becomes rough and red.

(c) Diarrhoea and poor digestion.

(d) Very little results in mental disorders and the disease pellagra (very rare in this country).

5. Effect of heat: Not lost in ordinary cooking.
6. In water — will dissolve (water soluble).

Vitamin C (Ascorbic acid)

1. Used for: (*a*) Growth.
   (*b*) Healing wounds and broken bones.
   (*c*) General health, e.g. vitality, skin, teeth.
   Note: The body cannot store Vitamin C, therefore a daily supply is necessary.
2. Found in: (*a*) Citrus fruits, e.g. oranges, lemons, grapefruit.
   (*b*) Blackcurrants, strawberries, gooseberries.
   (*c*) Cabbages, sprouts, new potatoes, tomatoes.
   (*d*) Rose-hip syrup.
   (*e*) Canned, A.F. Dried and frozen fruit and vegetables keep useful amounts.
3. Special (*a*) Babies and children.
   needs (*b*) Expectant and nursing mothers
   (*c*) Invalids.
4. Too little: (*a*) Children's growth slowed down.
   (*b*) Sore mouth and gums.
   (*c*) Feel tired and achey.
   (*d*) Wounds and broken bones heal slowly.
   (*e*) May get disease called scurvy.
5. Effect of (*a*) Some lost in cooking.
   heat: (*b*) Some lost when food is kept hot.
   (*c*) Some lost by oxidation (e.g. if source is cut or wilted).
   Loss reduced by:
   (*a*) Eating fruit and vegetables raw if possible.
   (*b*) Using fresh fruit and vegetables.
   (*c*) Avoiding crushing and bruising.
   (*d*) Soaking as little as possible.
   (*e*) Shredding and placing in small quantity of boiling water at once (lid on).
   (*f*) Dishing and serving immediately after cooking.
   (*g*) Using cooking water for gravy, soup, etc.
6. In water — dissolves easily in water (water soluble).

Vitamin D (Calciferol, sunshine vitamin)

1. Used for making strong bones and teeth.
   Note: The body can store Vitamin D in body fats.
2. Found in: (*a*) Fish liver oils.
   Oily fish, e.g. sardines, salmon, herrings.

14

Dairy foods — not a rich source but more in summer.
Vitaminised margarine.

(b) By the action of sunshine on the skin. (The layer of fat under the skin contains ERGOSTEROL which is converted to Vitamin D when the body is exposed to sunlight.)

3. Special (a) Babies and children.
   needs: (b) Expectant and nursing mothers.
4. Too little: (a) Children — bones remain soft (Rickets), teeth poor.
   Adults — bones may become soft and teeth poor.
5. Effect of heat: Not destroyed by ordinary cooking.
6. In water: Will not dissolve in water.
   Will dissolve in fat (called 'fat soluble').

Meal planning

General points to consider

1. Individual needs — age, sex, work, health.
2. Food values. Providing food from all food groups.
3. Time of year, time of day.
4. Variety in flavour, texture, colour, appearances and cooking methods.
5. Whether family or special occasion meal.
6. Number of people.
7. How much money to spend, time to prepare.
8. Cooking methods to consider, to use the oven or just the top of the cooker, automatic timing, etc.
9. Shopping, buying in season, storing, using food in rotation, planning for several days.
10. Capabilities of the person doing the cooking.

Infants and young children

Babies: Breast feeding usually best.
          Bottle feeding, must get advice from doctor or clinic.
          Orange juice, cod liver oil, etc. are important.
Up to 12 years: Period of rapid growth and activity.
1. Need well balanced diet, i.e.
   Protein — meat, milk, fish, eggs, cheese.
   Fresh fruit and vegetables.
   Dairy produce (with plenty of milk to drink).

Carbohydrate foods — to fill up, sweets in moderation (never just before meals).
2. Food with 'bite', e.g. apples, crusts, etc.
3. Meals should be regular and on time.
4. Avoid highly spiced foods.
5. Introduce new foods gradually.
6. Small children should have small cutlery, own place mat, etc.
7. Serve small portions to toddlers (more if asked for). Larger portions for older children.
8. Mealtimes should be happy times but small children need to be taught how to manage their cutlery, etc.

Food for small children must be easily digested and free from bones, gristle, etc.

Adolescents

Need food for growing and activity.
Appetites are large but a balanced diet is very important.
Food rich in iron is important, especially for girls.
Still need plenty of milk.
Should have fresh fruit and vegetables daily.

Adults

Manual workers:
(a) Need extra Calories (see page 18) provided by fats and carbohydrate foods.
(b) Also need extra vitamin B_1, to help digestion of carbohydrates.
(c) If working in a hot place, need extra salt and Vitamin C.
Sedentary workers:
(a) Should have less carbohydrate foods in diet, extra fruit and vegetables.
(b) Need easily digested food.
(c) Small meals more often, better than large meals.
Housewives:
(a) Need a balanced diet (must have enough protein).
(b) Iron rich foods are important.
(c) Regular meals better than several hasty 'tea and biscuits' snacks.
Expectant and Nursing Mothers:
(a) Should take advice of doctor or clinic regarding diet.
(b) Usually need extra protein, vitamins, iron and calcium.
(c) Need about one litre of milk a day as well as daily fresh fruit and vegetables.

Old people

Still need a well-balanced mixed diet.
Difficulties: (a) Money may be limited.
 (b) Digestion poor.
 (c) Cooking difficult.
 (d) Too miserable to bother.
   Need help to get necessary nutrients and regular meals. Also with shopping and preparation.

Packed meals

(a) Main meals should be well balanced, especially if the person only has a skimpy breakfast and evening snack.
(b) Always include a drink (could be hot soup in cold weather).
(c) Choose foods which are easy to pack and to carry.
(d) Useful foods include fresh fruit, salad, hard boiled eggs, cheese, cold meats, meat and fruit pasties, fruit cake.
(e) If taken every day packed meals should be varied as much as possible.
(f) Sedentary workers should not have a large amount of carbohydrate in the meal.
(g) Food should be appetising and well packed to prevent staleness and crushing. Plastic bags, boxes, foil, cling film, vacuum flasks, are all useful.
(h) Picnic meals can include almost any type of food. Picnic hampers, large wide-mouthed vacuum flasks and insulated boxes and bags are all useful, especially when travelling by car.

   Things like tin openers, salt, spoons, etc. must not be forgotten. In some cases water too may be required (if only for the dog).

Vegetarians

Two types:
(a) Strict vegetarians do not eat any animal food.
(b) Lacto-vegetarians do not eat meat, poultry or fish, but will eat milk, eggs, cheese.
Strict vegetarians — Difficulties:
(a) To supply essential amino acids, vitamins A, B_{12} and D, calcium, phosphorus, iron.
(b) To avoid bulky indigestible meals.
(c) To make varied, interesting meals.
(d) Cost.

Useful foods are:

Protein — Pulses, cereals, nuts, root vegetables.
Fat — Vegetable oils and margarine, nuts.
Calcium, iron, phosphorus — green vegetables and nuts.
Vitamin A — as carotene in vegetables.
Vitamin D — Vegetarian vitaminised margarine and sunshine.
For flavour — Vegetable extracts, herbs, spices, onions, tomatoes, mushrooms.

Health food shops and books will give advice and recipes.

Invalids

1. Obey the doctor's instructions.
2. Food and drink must be clean, fresh and best quality.
3. Serve food regularly and punctually.
4. Preparation and cooking should be done out of sight and smell of the sick room (when possible).
5. Serve easily digested foods. Avoid fried, greasy, highly flavoured and bulky meals.
6. Serve food attractively. Small portions, pretty china, clean cutlery.
7. Remove tray after the meal. Leave a drink, covered and within easy reach.

Liquid diet: Fruit juice, milk drinks, barley water, jelly.
Light diet: Milk and milk dishes, e.g. moulds, junkets, etc.
             Egg dishes, e.g. custards, scrambled, poached.
             White fish, steamed, grilled.
             Vitamin C, fruit and fruit drinks.
Convalescent diet:
             Body building foods — poultry, eggs, white fish, minced lean meat, milk drinks. Vitamin C fruit and vegetables (strained if necessary).

Don't serve: Pork, suet puddings, oily fish, shellfish (also see (5) above).
Note: Strained baby foods are very useful for invalid diets.

Calories

Calories (also called Kilocalories) measure:
1. The energy value of the food we eat.
2. The energy the body uses for its workings, e.g. heart beating, blood circulating, lungs breathing, maintenance of body temperature, etc.

Notes.

1. People usually put on weight if the Calorie value of the food they eat is more than the Calories used by the body.
2. People can usually slim if they
   (*a*) Cut down the Calorie value of their food but keep up their usual activity.
   (*b*) Increase their activity without increasing the Calorie value of their food.

Shopping for food

1. Meals should be planned as far ahead as possible.
2. Larder and refrigerator should be checked before shopping to save over-buying.
3. Buy food in season, usually best and cheapest.
4. Only buy large quantities of 'special offers' etc. if the family like the commodity.
5. Buy best quality food when money will allow.
6. Buy at clean shops (see section on food hygiene, p. 78).
7. Buy where the turnover is quick.
8. If you have a regular order the shops should be visited at intervals to check prices etc.
9. Take a shopping list.

Amounts to allow for each person

Meat	With bone 150 g	Fresh peas	150 g
	No bone 125 g	Potatoes	150 g
Fish	With bone 150 g	Fruit for stewing	125 g
	No bone 125 g	Rice for curry	25 g
Haricot beans	50 g	Puddings and pies	30 g flour
Runner beans	150 g	Junkets and blancmange	150 ml of milk
Greens	150 g	Fruit for pies	125 g
Carrots, parsnips,		Custard	150 ml of milk
swedes	150 g	Soup	300 ml

Meat

Sources of meat used in this country are:
1. Bullock — beef.
2. Sheep — lamb and mutton.
3. Pig — pork.
4. Rabbit.
5. Domestic birds — chickens, turkeys, geese, ducks.
6. Game birds — pheasant, partridge, grouse.

Structure

1. Lean is muscle tissue. Consists of bundles of fibres held together by connective tissue.

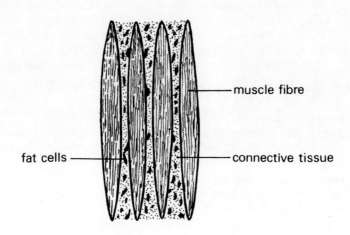

Diagram of muscle fibres

  (*a*) Older animals — thick long fibres — tougher meat.
  (*b*) Younger animals — thin short fibres — more tender meat.
  (*c*) More active muscles in any animal will give tougher meat, e.g. chicken legs, shin of beef.
2. Fat.
  (*a*) Some between muscle fibres of lean parts of meat (called 'invisible').
  (*b*) Some in layers under the skin.
  (*c*) Fat round important organs, e.g. suet round kidneys.

Food value

Animal protein (Myosin, globulin).
Fat.
Vitamins — Mainly B group, some A.
Mineral salts — Some sulphur, phosphorus, iron.
Water.
Extractives — give meat its flavour, help digestion but no food value.

Choosing

1. Good colour, lean and fat.
2. Fresh smell.
3. Flesh firm and elastic to touch.
4. Moist but not wet.
5. Fine even grain.
6. Not too much bone.

Effects of heat

1. Protein coagulates at 70°C and meat becomes firmer. Overheating hardens the proteins.
2. As the proteins shrink, juice is squeezed out. Overheating causes the meat to shrink too much.
3. Collagen becomes soluble gelatin, which allows muscle fibres to separate from each other and meat becomes tender. (Collagen is a protein of connective tissue).
4. Elastin is also a protein of connective tissue. It remains unchanged by heat so that the parts of the animal which have most elastin never become tender even with long cooking (e.g. the neck).
5. Bacteria are killed.
6. Fat near the surface melts.
7. The meat becomes more digestible.
8. The colour changes and taste improves.
9. Some vitamins B are destroyed by heat.

Notes

1. Basting (pouring fat over the meat) keeps meat moist, prevents over-shrinking and improves flavour. Covered roasting tins or cooking in foil has a similar effect to basting.
2. When cooking in foil
   (*a*) Add about 15 min. extra time.
   (*b*) Open foil for last 20 min. to brown outside of meat.
3. Frozen meat must be properly defrosted before cooking.

Methods of cooking

Roasting, grilling, frying, boiling, stewing, braising.

1. *Roasting*

   Beef — sirloin, top rump, rib, aitchbone.
   Lamb — shoulder, leg, best end of neck, breast.
   Pork — leg, loin, fillet, blade, spare rib.
   Veal — loin, fillet, breast.

Time: Beef: 15 min per 500 g + 20 min.
             Lamb: 20 min per 500 g + 20 min.
             Pork: 25 min per 500 g + 25 min.
             Veal: 25 min per 500 g + 25 min.

These times are approximate, e.g. 'thin' joints cook quicker than thicker ones.

2. Grilling and frying

(a) Both quick methods.
(b) Suitable for small tender cuts of meat, e.g. fillet and rump steaks, chops, cutlets, kidneys.
(c) Meat must be turned to prevent the outside becoming hard.
(d) Time of cooking depends on thickness and not on weight.

3. Boiling

(a) Suitable for:
        Beef — topside, silverside, brisket, ox tongue.
        Pork — ham, cheek, belly (pickled).
        Mutton — leg, middle neck.
(b) The meat is put into boiling water, which sets the outside protein. Water then simmered. Fibres become softened.
(c) Liquor useful for gravies and sauces unless very salty.

4. Stewing

(a) Useful for cheap cuts of meat, e.g.
        Beef — shin, neck, thin flank, chuck steak.
        Lamb or mutton — middle neck, scrag end of neck.
        Veal — breast, neck, knuckle.
(b) Long slow cooking (lid on).
(c) Meat sometimes fried first to improve flavour.
(d) Gravy used as part of dish, e.g. Brown stew.

5. Braising

(a) Useful for tougher cuts of meat not suitable for roasting.
(b) It combines stewing and roasting.
(c) Meat cooked on bed of vegetables (mirepoix) in strong saucepan (lid on). Stock added to come half way up meat.
(d) Cooking done first on top of stove, then in oven (or all in the oven).

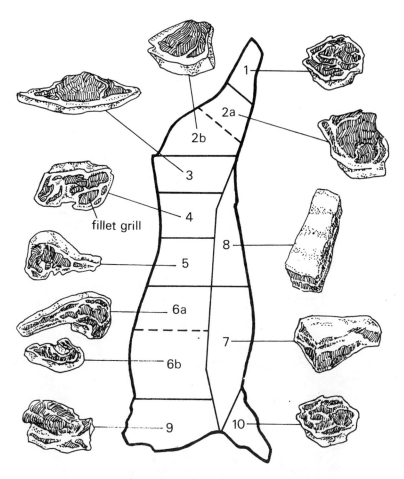

1. Leg or Shin–Stew or use for stocks and soups
2a. Topside–Pot roast or braise
2b. Silverside–Salt and boil or boil fresh
3. Rump–Roast or grill
4. Sirloin with Undercut–Roast
5. Wing Rib–Roast
6a. Forerib–Roast
6b. Shoulder Steak–Stew, use for pies and puddings
7. Brisket–Salt and boil or boil fresh
8. Flank–Salt and boil or boil fresh
9. Neck or clad sticking
10. Shin

Do you know the cuts of beef?

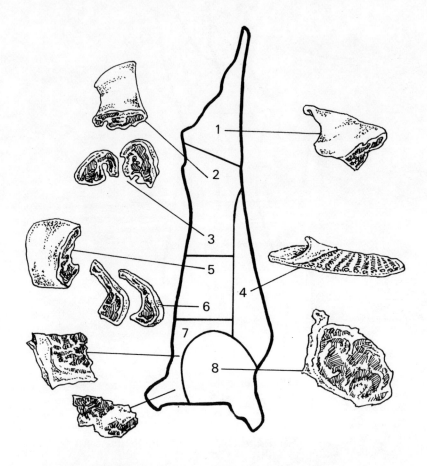

1. Leg—Roast
2 & 3. Loin—Roast in one piece or cut into chops and fry or grill
4. Breast—Stew
5 & 6. Best end of Neck—Roast or divide into chops and fry or grill
7. Middle Neck and Scrag End Neck—Stew
8. Shoulder—Roast

Do you know the cuts of mutton and lamb?

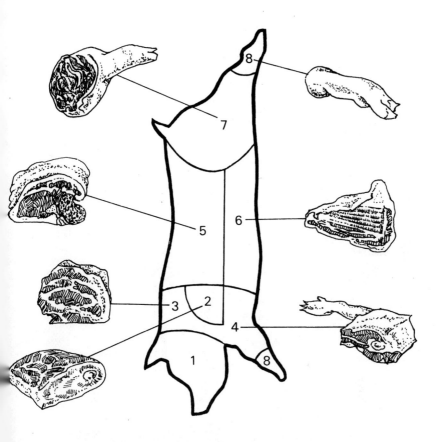

1. Head—Salt, boil and make into brawn
2 & 3. Spare Rib and Blade—Roast or cut into chops and grill or fry
4. Hand—Salt and boil
5. Loin with Kidney—Roast or cut into chops and fry or grill
6. Belly—Salt and boil or roast (slow method)
7. Leg—Roast or salt and boil
8. Foot—Salt and boil. Use with head for making brawn

Do you know the cuts of pork?

Offal

(a) Edible parts of the inside of animals, e.g. liver, heart, kidney, brain, tongue, sweedbreads, tripe.

(b) Must be very fresh and clean. Cook soon after buying.

Food value: (a) Animal protein.
               (b) Iron in liver and kidney.
               (c) Vitamin A (especially in liver).
               (d) Vitamin B group.

Methods of cooking:
               (a) Liver — fry, stew, braise, patés.
               (b) Kidney — fry, grill, stew, pies, soups.
               (c) Heart — roast, stew, braise.
               (d) Trip — stew.
               (e) Sweetbreads — fry, grill, steam, stew.

Chickens

Choosing — Plump breast, smooth legs, fresh smell, not discoloured.

Food value: (a) Animal protein.
               (b) Vitamin B group.
               (c) Iron.
               (d) Phosphorus.

Notes

(a) Usually easier to digest than meat.

(b) Not much fat — useful for invalids.

(c) May be roasted, boiled, casseroled, fried, grilled.

(d) Frozen chickens must be thawed according to directions. (Giblets usually in bag inside).

Accompaniments

1. *Roast meat*

Beef — Yorkshire pudding, horseradish sauce, mustard, thin gravy.
Lamb — mint sauce, thin gravy (thick if joint is stuffed).
Mutton — onion sauce, red currant jelly, thin gravy (thick if stuffed).
Pork — apple sauce, sage and onion stuffing, thick gravy.
Veal — bacon rolls, lemon slices, veal forcemeat stuffing, thick gravy.
Chicken — bread sauce, veal forcemeat, bacon rolls, thin gravy.

2. *Boiled meat*

Salt beef — carrot, turnip, onion, dumpling, gravy (strained cooking liquid).
Mutton — vegetables as for beef, caper sauce.

3. *Grilled or fried meat*

Grilled tomatoes, mushrooms, parsley butter, fried potatoes.

4. *Braised meat*

Vegetables cooked with meat (if liked), separate balls or cubes of carrots and swede, reduced cooking liquid.

5. *Stews*

Vegetables cooked with meat. Vegetables cooked separately, rice or potatoes (creamed or boiled). Thickened cooking liquid.

Milk

'Milk' means cow's milk to most people in this country but some people do use goat's milk.

In some countries people use the milk from asses, ewes, goats and reindeer.

Milk is often called the 'perfect food' but although it is excellent it is not quite perfect for human beings.

Composition

Solids: Protein — 3.29%
            Fat — 3.71%
            Carbohydrate — 4.7%   } 12.46%
            Minerals — 0.76%
Water: 87.54%

Food value

Animal protein — (chief protein is caseinogen).
Fat — (easily digested).
Carbohydrate — milk sugar (lactose).
Vitamins — A (more in summer), B group, D (small amount).
Minerals — rich in calcium and phosphorus.

But: (a) Lacks iron.   (d) Low in some of B groups.
           (b) Low in vit C (often none). (e) No roughage for adults.
           (c) Low in vit D.   (f) Easily contaminated.

Safe milk. Steps taken to make sure milk sold is clean and safe:

1. Cows must be healthy and kept under hygienic conditions.
2. Milk must be transported quickly and under ideal conditions.
3. Special rules for all milk-handlers.
4. Milk may be tested at any stage.
5. Milk processed to destroy harmful bacteria.

Grades of milk

Grades of milk	Definition	Process
Untreated	Milk which has not undergone any form of heat treatment.	Bottled under licence by farmer at dairy.
Pasteurised	Milk which has been subjected to mild heat treatment to destroy disease-causing bacteria.	Milk heated to 71°C for 15 seconds and then rapidly cooled to not more than 10°C.
Sterilised	Homogenised milk which has been heat treated in the bottle and vacuum-sealed.	Pre-heating, homogenisation, bottling and sealing. The filled bottles are then heated to 104°C–110°C for 20–30 min. and allowed to cool.
Ultra heat treated	Homogenised milk which has been subjected to ultra high temperature treatment — generally referred to as long-keeping milk.	Heating to 132°C for one second, destroying micro-organisms without producing undesirable chemical changes that would affect flavour.
Homogenised	Pasteurised milk processed to break up the fat globules and distribute them evenly throughout the milk.	Warm milk is forced through a fine aperture resulting in the breakup of the fat globules into small particles which do not rise to the surface but remain evenly suspended throughout the milk.
Channel Islands and South Devon	Milk from Jersey, Guernsey and South Devon breeds of cow with a minimum butterfat content of 4%.	Available untreated or pasteurised.

Storage of milk in the home

1. Never leave milk outside (loss of Vit C and riboflavin).
2. Keep cool and covered (best in fridge).
3. Always use clean jugs, etc.
4. Don't mix old and new milk.
5. Don't leave it near strong smelling foods or other substances.
6. Boil or scald to keep.

Milk in the diet

Serve as: milk drinks, with cereals, in puddings, moulds, jellies, junkets, custards, soups, sauces, cakes, etc.

Milk products

Cream, butter, cheese, yoghurt.
Skimmed — liquid and dried.
Condensed — evaporated with sugar added.
Evaporated — water reduced.
Dried — full cream or skimmed.
   Babies must not be given skimmed milk of any kind (unless a doctor said so for some reason).

Fish

Kinds of fish

1. White fish, e.g. cod, whiting, haddock, sole, halibut. Little or no fat (fat in liver).
2. Oily fish, e.g. herrings, mackerel, salmon, eel. Fat distributed in flesh, giving it a dark colour — more difficult to digest than white fish.
3. Shellfish, e.g. shrimps, crab, lobster, cockles. Fibres tough — indigestible.

Food value

Protein — animal.
Fat — oily fish — in flesh, white fish — in liver.
Calcium — useful amounts, especially if bones are eaten.
Phosphorus — useful amounts, especially if bones are eaten, also some potassium, fluorine, iodine, iron.
Vitamins — oily fish — A, D some B group. White fish — A (little in flesh) — D (in liver). Some B group.
Water.

Choosing

1. No unpleasant smell.
2. Flesh firm and moist.
3. Bright eyes and gills (eyes not sunken).
4. Plenty of scales.

Cooking

1. Frying: conserves flavour and nutritive value.
2. Steaming: for small pieces.
3. Grilling: conserves flavour and nutritive value.
4. Boiling: suitable for large fish.
5. Baking: conserves flavour — may be stuffed.
6. Sousing: (cooking in vinegar) e.g. herrings.

Effects of heat

Changes similar to those which occur when meat is cooked but there is less shrinkage because fish has less connective tissue.

Garnishing

Lemon, parsley, chopped egg, watercress.

Eggs

'Eggs' usually refer to hens' eggs although duck, goose and turkey eggs are quite often eaten, as well as the eggs of some lesser known birds.

Composition

Average egg weighs about 60 g.
Of the whole egg: shell = 10%, yolk = 30%, white = 60%.

Shell: (a) Consists of chalk.
          (b) Is porous (air and bacteria enter, water escapes).
Yolk: (a) Food store for chicken.
          (b) Richer than white, easily digested.
White: (a) Good food value.
          (b) No fat.
          (c) Easily digested.

Nutrients of whole egg

1. Animal protein.
2. Fat in yolk — emulsified — easily digested.

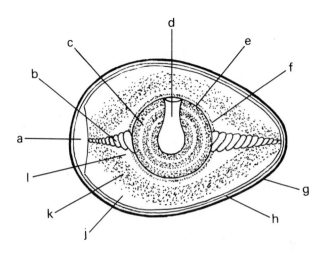

Diagram of fowl's egg.

(a) *air cell*, (b) *chalaza*, (c) *yolk*, (d) *germinal disc and white yolk*, (e) *vitelline membrane*, (f) *film of mucin*, (g) *shell*, (h) *shell membranes*, (j) *outer thin white*, (k) *thick white*, (l) *inner thin white*.

From *Testing of Eggs for Quality*, by permission of The Controller, H.M.S.O

3. Mineral   (*a*) Iron — a rich source.
    elements: (*b*) Useful amount of calcium.
             (*c*) Some sulphur, phosphorus.
4. Vitamins — A, some B group, D.

Eggs also contain quite a large amount of water, about 75% of whole.

Tests for freshness

1. Shell should be slightly rough.
2. When light is passed through, should be slightly transparent (bad eggs opaque). Candling test used.
3. Should feel heavy — stale eggs light (because moisture has evaporated from egg). Brine test used (50 g salt to $\frac{1}{2}$ litre of water).
4. When broken on to a saucer the yolk of a fresh egg is 'dome' shaped and firm and the white is thick and not watery.

Uses of eggs in cookery

1. As *main dish*: Use instead of meat and fish — also useful for some vegetarians, children and invalids.

2. *Thickening*, e.g. custards, sauces, soups.
3. *Binding*, e.g. croquettes, fish cakes, rissoles.
4. *Coating*, e.g. fish, scotch eggs.
5. *Enriching*, e.g. milk puddings, soups, potatoes.
6. *Lightening*, e.g. cakes, soufflés, meringues (whites).
7. *Emulsifier*, e.g. mayonnaise (one yolk can hold about 150 ml of olive oil in emulsion).
8. *Glaze*, e.g. gives shiny golden look to pastry.
9. *Garnish*: sieved or sliced, e.g. for dressed crab.

Methods of cooking

Boiling, poaching, frying, scrambling, baking, steaming (custards).

Effects of heat

1. Egg proteins coagulate (yolk at about 70°C, white at about 60°C).
2. Overheating causes toughness.
3. When eggs are added too quickly to hot liquids curdling results.
4. If boiled, custards and sauces etc. containing eggs will curdle.

   To prevent curdling use a double saucepan or a water bath. Remove a sauce from the heat before adding eggs.

Egg white foam

1. When egg white is whisked a foam is formed.
2. The protein (albumin) is stretched and dried by the whisking.
3. The foam consists of tiny bubbles of air surrounded by a film of stretched protein.
4. Too much heating causes the stability and volume to become less.
5. Various degrees of stiffness are used, meringues for example are whisked to the stiff-peak stage.
6. It takes longer to whisk egg whites which have just been taken out of the refrigerator.
7. The addition of sugar strengthens the foam and improves the flavour and texture. It also slows down foam formation.
8. The addition of acid increases the rate at which the protein coagulates. It also aids foam development and makes the foam more stable but more whisking is needed.
9. Foam stability and volume are lessened by the addition of milk, fat, oil, water, egg yolk and salt.

Cheese

Basic process of manufacture

1. Milk is clotted with rennet or acid (e.g. vinegar) or soured by bacteria.
2. Whey is strained off from curd.
3. Curd is salted and pressed (to remove last of whey).
4. Curd left to ripen. Flavour develops by action of bacteria and moulds.

Food value

(a) $\frac{1}{3}$ protein, $\frac{1}{3}$ fat, $\frac{1}{3}$ water.
(b) Calcium, Phosphorus.
(c) Vitamins A, D and riboflavin.

Good points

(a) Protein is animal.
(b) Rich source of calcium.
(c) Very compact food.
(d) Cheap protein food.

Some types of cheese

1. Hard — Cheddar, Cheshire, Double Gloucester, Parmesan.
2. Soft — Caerphilly, Camembert, Stilton, Gorgonzola.
3. Cream cheeses — mild flavour, do not keep long.
4. Processed — cheese ground to powder, melted with pasteurised milk, solidified, wrapped in foil.

To make cheese digestible

1. Grating or fine chopping (also proper chewing).
2. Never over-cook.
3. Serve with starchy foods, e.g. potatoes, bread, biscuits.
4. Season well, e.g. mustard.

Uses of cheese

1. Raw — in sandwiches, salads, and with soups.
2. Cooked: (a) Cheese pie, flan, soufflé, rarebit.
            (b) In sauces.
            (c) Cheese pastry and scones.

Cereals

1. Cereals are the seeds of cultivated grasses, e.g. wheat, oats, barley, rye, rice and maize.
2. Cereals are important foods, but because they contain so much starch they should be eaten with foods rich in protein and fat.
3. They are a cheap food for energy.

Food value

1. Carbohydrate — rich source.
2. Protein (vegetable) — useful amounts.
3. Fat — small amounts — wheat germ more.
4. Vitamin B group — good source but some lost in milling (most in germ).

Wheat

1. Most important cereal in this country.
2. Food value depends on amount of milling.
   White flour: contains about 70% of the grain.
   Wholemeal flour: contains about 90% of the grain (more sometimes).
   Germ flour: about 75% white flour mixed with 25% cooked germ.
   Starch reduced flour: much of the starch is washed out but gluten left in.
   Self-raising flour: white flour with fixed amount of raising agent added.

Wheat products

Semolina — made from endosperm of hard wheat.
   Used for puddings, thickening soups and some biscuits.
Pasta — also made from hard wheat. Made into paste with water.
   Drawn into tubes or moulded into shapes.
   e.g. Macaroni, spaghetti, noodles.
Shredded wheat and other breakfast cereals made from wheat.
Gluten is a protein. It can absorb water to make an elastic substance.
   This stretches and holds expanded gas when cooked.
   Strong or hard flours have strong gluten — good for bread making.
   Weak or soft flours have weaker gluten — good for cakes and biscuits.

Oats

Made into oatmeal, fine, medium or ground. Also rolled to make 'rolled oats' for porridge.
   Food value — Useful for protein, fat, carbohydrate, Vitamin B group.

Barley

Sold as pearl barley — may be used for thickening soups or as barley water.

Rice

Rice used in this country is mainly polished.

Used for milk puddings, savoury dishes. Also ground and used for cakes.

Food value— Mainly starch, poor in protein, fat and mineral elements.

Rice paper (used for base of macaroons) is not made of rice.

Maize

Called 'corn' in America. Cornflour is made from maize — useful for thickening, sauces, soups, stews and for blancmange.

Corn on the cob or sweet corn is used as a vegetable.

Arrowroot, sago, tapioca

These are not true cereals. They are almost 100% starch.
Arrowroot (from maranta plant). Used for puddings and thickening.
Sago (from sago palm). Used for milk puddings.
Tapioca (from cassava plant). Used for milk puddings.

Vegetables

Vegetables are important in the diet:
- (*a*) For essential vitamins and minerals.
- (*b*) For roughage.
- (*c*) For their flavour and colour.

Classes

1. Green vegetables (include leaves and flowers), e.g. cabbage, sprouts, spinach, cauliflower, lettuce.
2. Roots and tubers, e.g. carrots, parsnip, swedes, beetroot, potatoes, onions.
3. Stems, e.g. celery, seakale, chicory, asparagus.
4. Seeds and pods, e.g.
   - (*a*) Peas, broad beans.
   - (*b*) Runner beans.
5. Pulses, e.g. dried peas, beans, lentils.
6. Fruits, e.g. tomatoes, cucumbers, marrows.

Food value

1. Vegetable protein — some (most in pulses).
2. Carbohydrates:
   (*a*) Starch (potatoes).
   (*b*) Sugar (beetroot, onions, tomatoes).
   (*c*) Starch and sugar (peas, broad beans, pulses).
3. Mineral elements — some calcium and iron but body cannot always use it.
4. Vitamins: A — as carotene; rich sources are carrots and green vegetables.
   C — rich sources are green vegetables, tomatoes, new potatoes. Some in most vegetables.
   B group — a little in most vegetables. Pulses a rich source.
5. Water.

Choosing

1. Green — good colour, firm, crisp, medium size.
2. Root — firm, free from soil, no sprouting, no spade marks.

Freshly picked vegetables are best, if obtainable.

Cooking

1. Boiling — all vegetables (use water for gravy, etc.).
2. Baking — most vegetables, e.g. potatoes in jackets, stuffed marrows and cabbage leaves, tomatoes, cauliflower au gratin, etc.
3. Roasting, e.g. potatoes, carrots, parsnips, round the meat.
4. Grilling, e.g. tomatoes, mushrooms.
5. Frying, e.g.
   Deep fat — onion rings, chip potatoes, etc.
   Shallow fat — sauté potatoes, onions, tomatoes, mushrooms.
6. Braising, e.g. celery, onions, chicory.
7. Stewing, e.g. celery, mushrooms.
8. Conservative method — retains flavour and food value.

To preserve food value

1. Peel thinly — use sharp knife.
2. Prepare just before cooking.
3. Do not soak for long periods.
4. Bicarbonate of soda destroys Vitamins B — better not to use it.
5. Don't throw away dark outer leaves — cook them about five minutes before adding rest.

6. Cook for the shortest time.
7. Vegetables cut finely, small amount of liquid, tight fitting lid.

Serving

1. Toss in butter, e.g. peas, carrots, potatoes, etc.
2. Serve with sauce, e.g. cauliflower, beetroot, marrow, etc.
3. Sprinkle with chopped parsley, e.g. potatoes, carrots.

Pulses

1. Soak all night — add $\frac{1}{4}$ teaspoon of bicarbonate of soda dissolved in $\frac{1}{2}$ litre hot water for 200 g pulse (too much bicarbonate of soda destroys Vitamin B, but a little helps to soften the skin of pulses).
2. Rinse.
3. Cook thoroughly.
4. May be served alone, or in stews, etc.

Salads

1. May be: (*a*) A main dish — should contain some protein food.
   (*b*) An accompaniment to a dish, e.g. steak, scotch eggs.
   (*c*) Served as a first course to a meal.
   (*d*) Used in sandwiches, rolls etc.
2. They should:
   (*a*) Contain fresh, clean, crisp ingredients.
   (*b*) Be arranged attractively.
3. Salad dressings add flavour and food value, aid digestion.
4. May contain:
   (*a*) Raw or cooked vegetables (green and root).
   (*b*) Fruit — fresh and dried.
   (*c*) Nuts.
   (*d*) Gherkins, pickles, chutneys.
   (*e*) Protein foods.
   (*f*) Added flavouring such as garlic, lemon juice etc.
5. Preparation:
   (*a*) Some vegetables can be prepared and put in the salad compartment of the refrigerator.
   If no refrigerator or if plate salads are being served they should not be prepared too far in advance.
   (*b*) Prepared salads should not be left in a warm place before serving.

(c) All ingredients must be very clean, e.g.
Vegetables washed under a running tap and drained.
Dried fruit washed and dried.
Unpeeled fruit must be washed and dried.
(d) Grating, chopping, slicing must be done neatly.
(e) Salads should be arranged attractively but not handled more than necessary.

6. Salad dressing may be made or bought.
Some kinds: French dressing.   Mayonnaise.
                Salad cream.   Vinaigrette.

Fruit

Eaten mainly for refreshing flavour, sweetness and in some cases, Vitamin C.

Food value

1. Very small amounts of vegetable protein, fat.
2. Some carbohydrate (as sugar in ripe fruit).
3. Small amount of iron and calcium in dried fruits.
4. Vitamin C — citrus fruits, rose hips, blackcurrants, etc.
   Vitamin A — apricots, peaches, tomatoes.

Fruits also contain 'fruit acids' — which
   (a) Helps the laxative action of fruit.
   (b) Helps jam set (with pectin).

Choosing

Fruit should be eaten when just ripe; under-ripe is difficult to digest, over-ripe upsets digestion.

Cooking

Stewing, baking (apples), frying (banana/pineapple/apple fritters).
   Also used for puddings, pies, fruit salads, fools, etc.

Water

1. Used for:
   (a) All body fluids.

(b) Digestion of food.

(c) Removing waste matter.

(d) Regulating body temperature.

(e) Lubricating joints and membranes.

Notes

(a) Water is vital to life.

(b) About two-thirds of body is made up of water.
It is continually lost through:
The lungs (breathing out).   The kidneys (urine).
The skin (perspiration).   The bowels (faeces).

2. Sources: (a) Water and other drinks.

(b) Food.

(c) Oxidation of energy foods.

About 1.4 litres of liquid should be drunk a day.

Gelatine

The gelatine sold in the shops is obtained from bones, hooves, etc. of young animals. It is purified and dried. It is usually sold as powdered gelatine.

Food value

1. A protein food but lacks four of the essential amino acids.
2. When mixed with other food containing incomplete proteins the nutritive value of both is increased.
3. Used in invalid cookery, especially gastric illnesses.
4. Helps to make appetising dishes when used with nourishing foods, e.g. eggs, milk, fruit, meat.

Notes on using gelatine

1. Measure correctly (usually 10 g to $\frac{1}{2}$ litre) or buy packets containing little envelopes ready measured.
2. Dissolve in a little cold or warm water (not boiling).
3. Never boil (gives it a gluey flavour and lessens setting power).
4. Add to a mixture by pouring slowly from a height and stirring.
5. Pour gelatine mixtures into moulds when cold and beginning to thicken.
6. Use for milk jellies, flan glaze, meat and vegetable moulds, cold soufflés, etc.

Methods of cooking

Main reasons for cooking food

1. To make it safe to eat — kill harmful bacteria.
2. To make it digestible.
3. To make it attractive to look at and taste.

Main methods of cooking food

1. Boiling, stewing, steaming, braising.
2. Grilling, baking, roasting, frying.

The heat is applied to the food as follows:
(*a*) Directly with or without extra fat (roasting, grilling, baking).
(*b*) With water (boiling, stewing, braising).
(*c*) With fat (frying).

In (*a*), (*b*) and (*c*) the heat is applied to the outside of the food.
In microwave cooking the heat is generated within the food.

Boiling

1. Food put into boiling water — then simmered until tender.
2. Suitable foods — meat, bacon, ham, fish, vegetables.

Stewing

1. Long, slow moist method. Liquid just simmers.
2. Liquid — water, stock, milk, syrup.
3. In pan on top of stove — in casserole in oven. (Lid on).
4. Advantages:
   (*a*) Cheap cuts of meat may be used.
   (*b*) Little loss of nutrients and flavour (in liquid).
   (*c*) Little fuel used.
   (*d*) Doesn't need much attention.
5. Foods suitable — cheap cuts of meat, fruit, fresh or dried.

Steaming

1. Moist method — food cooks in steam rising from boiling water.
2. Direct   (*a*) In a steamer.
   contact: (*b*) In a pan of boiling water.
   Foods — Puddings, custards, fish, potatoes, root vegetables.

3. Indirect contact — food between two plates over a pan of boiling water.
4. Food may be in a basin, wrapped in foil or left free.
5. Advantages:
        (*a*) Food more digestible.
        (*b*) Little loss of nutrients.
        (*c*) Puddings lighter.
        (*d*) Food not broken.
        (*e*) Economical on fuel with careful planning.
6. Rules: (*a*) Water must be kept boiling. Keep a kettle of boiling water handy for refilling.
        (*b*) Lid and steamer sections must fit well to prevent steam escaping.
        (*c*) Boil water in pan before food is put in.

Pressure cooking

1. Steam used under high pressure.
2. High temperature, e.g. with 15 lb pressure, temperature is 121°C (water boils at 100°C).
3. Tightly fitting lid.
4. Cooks very quickly.
5. Important that instructions are followed exactly.

Roasting (see Meat section p. 19)

Baking

1. Cooking in the oven — radiant heat — no fat.
2. Foods suitable — bread, cakes, puddings, potatoes (in jackets), fruit (e.g. baked apples).

Grilling (see also Meat section p. 19)

1. Quick method by radiant heat.
2. Surface of food seals quickly — flavour not lost.
3. Suitable for meat, fish, chicken joints, tomatoes, mushrooms, savouries on toast, toast alone.

Frying

1. Quick method of cooking.
2. Surface of food seals quickly — flavour not lost.
3. Suitable fats — lard, clarified dripping, cooking fats and oils.

4. Two methods of frying:
   (a) Shallow frying. (b) Deep fat frying.

Shallow frying

1. Foods rich in fat may be fried with no extra fat, e.g. bacon, sausages.
2. Little fat for frying, e.g. eggs, pancakes, mushrooms (liver, lean steak little more).
3. Fat half way up sides of food — fish cakes, rissoles, thick fish.

Deep fat frying

1. Food is covered by fat.
2. Fat pan about half full of fat.
3. Need deep heavy pan.
4. Frying basket necessary for some foods.
5. Most foods are coated with one of the following:
   (a) Seasoned flour.   (c) Batters.
   (b) Flour, egg and breadcrumbs.   (d) Pastry.

Coating seals and protects food.

Rules for frying

1. Use clean fat at the correct temperature (thermometer helpful.)
2. Don't put too much food in the pan when deep frying.
3. Never drop food in.
4. Drain fried food on absorbent paper.
5. Strain fat after use.

Notes

1. Modern fats may not give off a 'haze' until they are too hot for frying.
2. 'Smoke point' is the temperature at which fat or oil gives off a bluish smoke (lard 171°C, cottonseed oil 210°C).
3. 'Flash point' is the temperature at which the vapour above the fat or oil will ignite.
4. 'Fire point' is the temperature at which fat or oil will support continued combustion.

Rancidity

1. Fats and oils become rancid is they are stored too long. Rancidity is hastened by the addition of heat, moisture, oxygen and light.
2. Manufacturers add antioxidants to fats and oils to keep them fresh longer.

Microwave cookery

This method of cooking is sometimes called High-frequency Heating and involves the use of electromagnetic radiation.

Advantages: 1. Quick method of cooking.
2. Can be used instead of keeping food hot for long periods. Less flavour and nutritional value lost.

Disadvan-   1. Very expensive.
tages: 2. Food does not brown on outside.
3. Cooking times must be carefully controlled.

Prepared foods from the deep freeze can be defrosted in the microwave oven and then cooked. It is safer not to cook from frozen in one step because the food may contain isolated cold spots.

Fats used in cooking

Animal

Butter. Made by churning separated cream. Contains about 85% fat. The rest is water. Some Vitamin A and D. Easily digested. May be used for cakes, biscuits, pastry etc. Also in sauces, for tossing vegetables, etc.

Lard. Fat from pigs. Soft and white. 100% fat. Has low melting point. Used for pastry (sometimes with margarine) and for frying.

Suet. The hard fat round internal organs of animals, e.g. kidneys of ox and sheep. Beef suet usually used. Shredded suet very useful but more expensive. Used for suet pastry, making puddings, e.g. steak and kidney pudding, Christmas pudding.

Dripping. Fat which has dripped whilst meat is cooking. Contains water and meat extracts, therefore likely to go rancid. Used for frying, sometimes for cakes and pastry (clarify before using).

Vegetable

Margarine. May be made from all vegetable fats (from nuts, seeds, etc.) or vegetable and animal fat. Vitamins A and D added (by law). Used for cakes, biscuits, pastry and puddings.

Olive oil. An expensive vegetable oil. Valued for its flavour. Not used much in this country. Often used in salad dressings.

Frying and cooking oils. Many brands on sale. Used for frying as well as for pastry, cakes, etc.

Cooking fats. Usually white fats. Some very soft texture (no creaming necessary). Used for cakes, pastries, frying etc. Directions on packets or in manufacturers' recipe books.

Fats used in cake-making

Fats used for making cakes must be efficient regarding creaming, emulsifying and shortening.

1. *Creaming*

The fat must be capable of incorporating air bubbles when beaten.

2. *Emulsifying*

(*a*) When the fat and sugar have been creamed egg is added and an emulsion is produced.

(*b*) 'High ratio' fats (or 'super-clycerinated' fats) contain an emulsifying agent (usually glycerol monostearate).
    The emulsion is made stable by the lecithin in the egg and the glycerol monostearate.

(*c*) Because the emulsion is stable more water can be emulsified with the fat. This means more sugar can be used and cakes high in sugar and moisture can be made.

(*d*) In a given recipe less 'high ratio' fat is required than normal fat.

3. *Shortening*

(*a*) Fat coats the starch and gluten of flour with an oily film. This breaks up the structure of the cake because it prevents a tough mass forming. The cake then has a 'short' crumb which makes the cake tender instead of a hard mass.

(*b*) A soft fat coats the flour better than a hard fat.

(*c*) Clycerol monostearate helps to improve the shortening power of the fat.

Starch and its uses in cookery

1. Starch is formed as granules in small bodies called leucoplasts.
2. The properties and appearance of the granules are characteristic for each plant.
3. Starch cannot be digested until it is cooked.

4. When the starch is cooked the cellulose cell walls are softened and the starch becomes digestible.
5. Starches are insoluble in cold water.
6. When heated with water the starch granules take up water and swell. This is called gelatinisation.
7. Whisking and stirring while heating facilitates gelatinisation.

Uses of starch in cookery include:

1. Bread, cakes, biscuits, scones, pastry, puddings, etc.
2. Milk puddings, e.g. rice, tapioca, semolina, blancmange.
3. For thickening gravy, sauces, stews, soups.
4. For binding, e.g. coatings for fish, fish cakes, croquettes.
5. For making pasta, e.g. macaroni, spaghetti, noodles.

Uses of sugar in cookery

1. As a sweetening agent.
2. In preservation — jams, jellies, canned and bottled fruit, freezing, chutneys, etc.
3. To make sweets, chocolate and icings.
4. To lighten mixtures because it helps food to trap air.
5. In the form of caramel to flavour and colour food.
6. To act as a substrate (the substance on which an enzyme acts) for yeasts in fermentation reactions.
7. To give a brown crust to baked foods.
8. In the making of meringues.

Raising agents

1. Gases expand when heated.
2. To make cake and bread mixtures light a gas must be introduced.
3. The gases used are Air and Carbon Dioxide.
4. The gases are introduced before baking by
   (*a*) mechanical means;   (*b*) chemical means.

Air

Introduced by:
1. Sieving the flour.
2. Rubbing fat into flour.
3. Creaming fat and sugar.
4. Whisking whole eggs and sugar.

5. Adding whisked white of egg.
6. Beating the mixtures, e.g. batters.
7. Folding and rolling,
   e.g. rough puff and flaky pastry.
8. Kneading.

Carbon dioxide

Introduced by:
1. Bicarbonate of soda. (a) Alone.
   (b) With an acid.
2. Yeast.

Bicarbonate of soda $2NaHCO_3$ (used alone)

Equation is: $2NaHCO_3$
on heating $\rightarrow Na_2CO_3 + H_2O + CO_2$
but Na_2CO_3 (washing soda) (a) Gives unpleasant taste.
(b) Yellow colour.

Therefore bicarbonate of soda is only used by itself for strong flavoured dark mixtures, e.g. gingerbread, parkin.

Bicarbonate of soda (with an acid)

Acids used: Cream of tartar
Tartaric acid $\left.\right\}$ No unpleasant
Sour milk taste or colour
Vinegar or lemon juice

Baking powder (usually made commercially)

Made up of: 25 g Bicarbonate of soda $\left.\right\}$ + 25 g Rice flour
50 g Cream of tartar (to absorb moisture)

As already stated no unpleasant taste is produced and no colour.

Self raising flour

1. A mixture of soft cake flour and raising agent.
2. Not suitable for all mixtures.

Steam (also a raising agent)

1. Steam is produced when the liquid used in a mixture reaches boiling point during cooking.

2. The steam rises up in the mixture and makes the mixture rise too.
   Oven heat sets the mixture.
3. To make use of steam as a raising agent two things are needed:
   (*a*) Plenty of liquid in the mixture.
   (*b*) A high temperature.
4. Some mixtures raised by steam are:
   Batters, e.g. Yorkshire pudding.
   Choux, rough puff and flaky pastries.

Yeast

1. Yeast is a living plant.
2. When fermented it produces carbon dioxide.
3. Yeast ferments when it is given
   (*a*) Food — sugar, flour.
   (*b*) Warmth
   (*c*) Liquid — water or milk.

High temperature kills yeast. Being cold slows down its activity.

Bread

Ingredients

1. Flour: Strong flour (good supply of gluten).
             Wholemeal, white, Hovis, starch reduced.
             Self-raising not suitable.
2. Yeast: Compressed usually used. Keep in cold place 2–3 days.
             Dried yeast, more concentrated.
3. Salt improves flavour.
4. Sugar used to be added to yeast — now considered too drastic.
5. Fat — added to rich doughs — slows down the action of yeast — more
   yeast necessary or longer rising.
6. Liquid — water, milk or a mixture of both. Must be lukewarm
   ($\frac{1}{3}$ boiling liquid + $\frac{2}{3}$ cold).
7. Eggs, fruit, flavourings added to richer mixtures.

Proportions (for **basic recipe**)

(*a*) 15 g yeast to 500 g flour.
(*b*) 20 g yeast to 700–750 g flour.
(*c*) 25 g yeast to 1–1$\frac{1}{2}$ kg flour.

Notes on making

1. Ingredients for basic recipe: 500 g plain flour, 15 g yeast, 1 level teaspoonful sugar, 2 level teaspoonfuls salt, 300 ml liquid.
2. Steps in general method of bread-making:
   Creaming — Yeast creamed with little water, then rest of water whisked with creamed yeast.
   Sponging — Yeast mixture poured on to flour and salt.
   Flour sprinkled on top. Bowl left in warm place until covered with bubbles.
   Mixing — Mixed well with hand.
   Kneading (1) — Until dough smooth (in bowl).
   Rising — Dough covered and left in warm place.
   Kneading (2) — On board until texture is even.
   Shaping — To fit tins (about $\frac{1}{2}$ full).
   Proving — Covered. Left in warm place until double its size.
   Baking — Electric 450°F, 230°C, Gas Mark 8 for 10 min.
   　　　　 Electric 375°F, 190°C, Gas Mark 5 until cooked.
3. To test — Tap bottom and sides of loaf — should sound hollow.
4. Quick method — Dough mixed, kneaded, put in tins to rise, baked.
5. Everything must be kept warm when making bread.
6. Variations: (*a*) Basic recipe — Brown or wholemeal bread, dinner rolls, Sally Lunn.
   　　　　　　 (*b*) Richer recipes — Currant bread, Hot Cross Buns, Chelsea buns, etc.

Stock

1. Stock is the liquid in which meat bones, vegetables or fish bones and trimmings have been simmered for a long time.
2. It contains little food value but extractives stimulate the appetite.
3. Important in making well-flavoured sauces, soups and gravies.

Notes on making stock

1. All the ingredients must be fresh and clean.
2. Strong deep pan with a well fitting lid necessary.
3. Meat cut up small (no fat). Vegetables rough chopped.
4. Balanced proportion of ingredients. No vegetable flavour should stand out.
5. Foods suitable.
   　　　　 (*a*) Cooked and raw meat and bones. Gristle and skin. Giblets. Bacon rinds.

      (*b*) Bones and trimming of white fish — Fish stock.

      (*c*) Liquid in which meat or fowl has been cooked (or liquid fish cooked in, for fish stock).

      (*d*) Vegetables, vegetable scraps and vegetable water.

6. Foods not suitable.

      (*a*) Starchy foods, e.g. bread, potatoes, barley (make stock sour).

      (*b*) Green vegetables or their water (gives stock bitter flavour).

      (*c*) Turnips.

      (*d*) Salty liquor, e.g. from salt meat.

7. Scum must be removed as it comes to the top.

8. Stock should not be left in pan overnight.

9. Stock cubes are convenient and better than water.

10. If stock is kept more than 24 hours reheat daily by bringing to boil quickly and keep boiling for at least 15 minutes.

Soups

1. Not much food value except meat soups.

2. Chief   (*a*) Stimulate digestive juices.
   value: (*b*) Warming in cold weather.
          (*c*) Useful for invalids.

Classes

1. Broths: Chicken, Scotch, Mutton.
2. Purées: Potato, Pea, Lentil, Celery, Tomato.
3. Clear soups (consommés).
4. Cream soups (thickened).
5. Fish soups (bisques).

Notes on soup making

1. Broths — made from meat, vegetables, meat and vegetables. Cereals added, e.g. pearl barley.

2. Purées: (*a*) Vegetables usually sieved before serving.
         (*b*) Thickened with flour or cornflour (potato and lentil may not need thickening).
         (*c*) Milk or cream sometimes added before serving.

3. Soups   (*a*) Free from grease.
  should be:(*b*) Good colour and flavour.
         (*c*) Correct consistency.

4. Accompaniments, e.g. for Purées — croûtons; for Minestrone — grated cheese.

Sauces

1. A sauce is a well-flavoured liquid and is usually thickened.
2. Used to add flavour to dull dishes and to add new flavour.
3. Add colour to dishes.
4. Improve appearance and texture.
5. Bind food together, e.g. rissoles, croquettes.
6. Add nutritive value, e.g. add milk, eggs.
7. Counteract the richness of some foods, e.g. apple sauce with pork.
8. Should be:
   - (*a*) Well flavoured.
   - (*b*) Suitable for dish.
   - (*c*) Made of ingredients which blend well.
   - (*d*) Have a distinctive flavour.
   - (*e*) Smooth, glossy, cooked, good colour and correct consistency.

Classes

1. Made with a roux base — white or brown.
2. Blended.
3. Cooked egg sauces.
4. Unclassified.

Roux sauce

1. Ingredients: Equal quantities of flour and fat. Liquid: stock, water, milk.
2. Consistency:
   - (*a*) Pouring.
   - (*b*) Coating.
   - (*c*) Binding (Panada).
3. Proportions:
   Pouring — 25 g fat, 25 g flour, 500 ml liquid.
   Coating — 50 g fat, 50 g flour, 500 ml liquid.
   Panada — 100 g fat, 100 g flour, 500 ml liquid.

Notes on making white sauce (roux method)

1. Fat melted in pan.
2. Flour added — stirred over gentle heat about three minutes (not browned).
3. Removed from heat — liquid added gradually whilst stirring.
4. Brought to boil, cooked until thickened, three to five minutes (stirred all the time).
5. Checked for consistency and seasoning.

Variations

Cheese — 50 g grated.

Parsley — 1 tablespoonful, finely chopped.
Mustard — 2 level teaspoonfuls dry mustard.
Onion — 200 g cooked onion.
Hard boiled egg — 1 hard boiled egg, chopped.
Anchovy — 2 teaspoonfuls anchovy essence.

Brown sauce

1. Ingredients: Flour, dripping, stock, carrots, onion, seasoning (tomato purée, bacon, mushroom stalks sometimes added).
2. Proportions: 20 g flour, 20 g dripping, 250 ml stock.

Notes on making brown sauce

1. Fat heated, vegetables fried until brown.
2. Flour stirred in. Cooked until brown.
3. Removed from heat — stock added gradually whilst stirring.
4. Brought to boil — then simmered about thirty minutes.
5. Skimmed once or twice.
6. Strained.
7. Checked for consistency, flavour and seasoning.
8. Reheated.

Blended sauces

1. Proportions: Pouring — 15 g cornflour to 250 ml milk.
   Coating — 20 cornflour to 250 ml milk.
2. May be sweet or savoury.
3. Method: (*a*) Cornflour and little liquid blended in basin.
   (*b*) Rest of liquid boiled and poured on to blended cornflour whilst stirring.
   (*c*) Mixture boiled for 3 to five minutes, until thickened and cooked.
   (*d*) Sugar or seasoning added.
4. Thickening may also be custard powder, arrowroot etc.

Variations

Chocolate: ½–1 level teaspoon chocolate powder added to cornflour.
  Coffee: 1 teaspoonful coffee essence.

Cooked egg sauces

1. Types: Custard, Hollandaise.
2. Important to heat the egg to point of thickening without curdling.

3. Should be heated until the mixture coats the back of the spoon.
4. They thicken on cooling.
5. Overheating causes curdling. Underheating results in egg separating from liquid on standing.

Batters

1. A mixture of plain flour, milk or water and usually egg.
2. The ingredients are beaten together until smooth.
3. Air is incorporated during beating.
4. The air expands when heated, making the mixture light.

Types of batter

1. Thin batter — pancakes, Yorkshire pudding and toad in the hole.
2. Coating batter — for coating fish or meat.
3. Fritter batter — for sweet or savoury fritters, kromeskies, etc.

Proportions

Thin: 1 egg, 100 g flour, 250 ml milk, $\frac{1}{4}$ teaspoon salt.
   Coating: 1 egg, 100 g flour, 150 ml milk, $\frac{1}{4}$ teaspoon salt.
Fritter: 1 egg white, 50 g flour, 3–4 tablespoons tepid water, 1 dessert-spoon salad oil, $\frac{1}{8}$ teaspoonful salt.

Notes on making basic recipe

1. Flour and salt sieved into bowl.
2. Egg in centre of flour.
3. Add half liquid — stir until smooth.
4. Add rest of liquid gradually — keep stirring.
5. Beat or whisk well.

Notes on using

1. Food coated must be dry.
2. Yorkshire pudding poured into hot fat.
3. Pancakes — nonstick pan best. Batter to cover pan thinly.
4. Drop scones — drop spoonfuls of batter on to greased girdle, hot plate or thick pan.

Re-heated food (réchauffés)

The term 'réchauffé' refers to any food which has been cooked, allowed to cool and is then reheated. The left-over food may be made into a completely different dish.

General rules for using left overs:

1. Immediately after a meal left overs must be:
   (*a*) Cooled quickly.
   (*b*) Put into clean covered containers.
   (*c*) Kept cool, e.g. in a refrigerator.
2. Before using, examine the left-over food to make sure it is perfectly fresh.
3. When possible divide the food up finely so that it can be reheated as quickly as possible, e.g. mash potatoes, flake fish, mince meat.
   Sometimes it's easier to do this before the food is cooled and put away.
4. Reheat protein foods quickly to prevent hardening (see also 'Food' p. 79).
5. Cook raw ingredients before adding, e.g. carrots, onions, etc.
6. Add extra flavour, e.g. seasoning, onion, tomato, mushrooms, curry powder, herbs, etc.
7. Add extra moisture, e.g. sauce, gravy, but take care these are quite fresh to prevent food poisoning.
8. To prevent overcooking food may be protected by:
   (*a*) Covering with potatoes, e.g. shepherds' pie.
   (*b*) Coating with egg and breadcrumbs, e.g. fish cakes.
   (*c*) Dipping in batter, e.g. fritters.
   (*d*) Covering with pastry, e.g. pasties.
9. Add Vitamin C to the meal by serving vegetables or fruit rich in vitamin C.
10. Don't reheat food a second time.

Some re-heated dishes

Meat: Shepherds' pie, curried meat, fritters, rissoles.
Fish: Fish cakes, fish pie, kedgeree.
Vegetables: 'Bubble and squeak'. Potatoes: potato cakes, and on shepherds' pie and fish pies.

Cakes

Main ingredients used are flour, fat, sugar, eggs, fruit, raising agent.

Flour: (*a*) Plain + baking powder.
           (*b*) Self raising.
           (*c*) No raising agent as a rule when using equal weight (or more) eggs to flour.

Fat: Margarine, butter, clarified dripping, cooking fats.

Sugar: Castor or moist brown. Granulated suitable for rubbed-in cakes.

Eggs: (*a*) Recipes usually refer to hen's eggs.

           (*b*) Should be fresh.

Fruit: (*a*) Clean and dry.

           (*b*) Glacé cherries — washed and dried.

Flavouring:(*a*) Dry, e.g. cocoa — sieve with flour.

           (*b*) Essences — beaten with eggs.

Liquid: (*a*) Milk or water for rubbed-in cakes.

           (*b*) Other methods — only if stated in recipe.

Types of cakes

1. Plain — $\frac{1}{2}$ or less fat to flour — Rubbing-in method.
2. Rich — More than $\frac{1}{2}$ fat to flour — Creaming method.
3. Sponges — No fat — Whisking method.
4. Gingerbread — Melting method.

Notes on making

Rubbing in

1. Flour, baking powder, salt sieved. (Very fine flour need not be sieved.)
2. Fat rubbed into flour.
3. Sugar and fruit stirred in.
4. Egg and other liquid stirred in to required consistency.
5. Baking: Small cakes — 400°F, 200°C (Gas Mark 6).

                Large cakes — 350°F–375°F, 180°C–190°C (Gas Mark 4–5).
6. Uses — Rock cakes, raspberry buns, large cakes.

Creaming

1. Flour, baking powder, salt sieved (rich fruit — plain flour).
2. Fat and sugar creamed.
3. Egg added little at a time (beat well).
4. Fruit stirred in.
5. Flour folded in gradually.
6. Put into prepared tins.
7. Baking: Small cakes — 375°F, 190°C (Gas Mark 5).

                Large cakes — 350°F–375°F, 180°C–190°C (Gas Mark 4–5).

                Fruit cakes — 300°F–350°F, 150°C–180°C (Gas Mark 2–4).

Whisking

1. General proportions: 1 egg and 25 g castor sugar to 25 g plain flour.
2. Flour sieved.
3. Eggs and sugar whisked over hot water (10–15 min.).
4. Whisking continued away from heat until very thick.
5. Flour folded in lightly — metal spoon.
6. Pour into prepared tins.
7. Baking: Small — 400°F, 200°C (Gas Mark 6).
             Swiss roll — 425°F, 220°C (Gas Mark 7).
             Sponge sandwich — 375°F, 190°C (Gas Mark 5) (reduced to 325°F, 170°C, Gas Mark 3, if necessary.)
8. Uses — Sponge drops and fingers, swiss roll, sponge sandwich.

Melting

1. General proportions:
   (*a*) $\frac{1}{3}$–$\frac{1}{2}$ fat and sugar to plain flour.
   (*b*) $\frac{1}{3}$–$\frac{3}{4}$ syrup to flour.
   (*c*) To 500 g of flour — 2 eggs, 2 level teaspoonfuls ginger or spice, 1 level teaspoonful bicarbonate of soda, or 2 level teaspoonfuls baking powder, 250 ml milk or water.
2. Flour, spices, raising agent sieved into mixing bowl.
3. Fat, sugar, syrup warmed gently in pan.
4. Melted mixture + liquid added to flour etc.
5. Mix quickly and well.
6. Pour into prepared tin.
7. Baking — 325°F–350°F, 170°C–180°C (Gas Mark 3–4).
   Reduce temperature to finish.
8. Uses — Gingerbread, malt loaf, parkin.

General notes

1. Tests for cooking:
             (*a*) Evenly coloured.
             (*b*) Firm when pressed lightly.
             (*c*) Large cakes shrunk a little from sides of tin.
             (*d*) No sound of hissing.
2. Storing: (*a*) Cool.
             (*b*) Put in tin lined with greaseproof.
             (*c*) Lid must be tight fitting.
   Plain cakes — about 2–3 days. Rich cakes — several days.
   Rich fruit cakes — several weeks. Fatless sponge — best eaten same day. Gingerbread best kept a day before cutting.

3. Cooling: (*a*) Plain and rich, leave in tin a few minutes before removing. Rich fruit, cool in tin.

   Gingerbread, take out whilst hot.

   (*b*) When taken out of tins put on cooling tray.

   (*c*) Don't stand cooling tray in a draught.

4. Curdling: Caused by adding egg too quickly. Cold egg cools fat, fat separates.

   To prevent — add egg at room temperature gradually.

   To correct — stir in a little flour from the recipe.

Pastry

1. Main ingredients used are flour, fat and water.
2. Eggs, sugar, cheese may be used to make rich pastries.

Flour. Plain flour should be used except:

   (*a*) For suet pastry.

   (*b*) For short-crust, if less than half fat to flour is used.

Fat. Margarine, lard, mixture of margine and lard, butter, dripping — for savoury dishes usually.

Liquid. Cold water. Egg yolk for richer pastries.

Raising agent. (*a*) Air usually.

   (*b*) Also baking powder for 2(*a*) and 2(*b*).

   Salt usually added to bring out flavour. (2 level teaspoonfuls to 500 g of flour.)

3. Fat is incorporated in the following ways:

   (*a*) Rubbed in to flour — Short crust.

   (*b*) Shredded and mixed with the flour — Suet crust.

   (*c*) Rough chopped, mixed with flour, then rolled in — Rough puff.

   (*d*) Laid on pastry in small pats, then rolled in — Flaky pastry.

4. Cooking: (*a*) Air expands.

   (*b*) Gluten absorbs water, stretches, is pushed up by expanded air and sets.

   (*c*) Starch grains swell, burst and absorb fat.

   (*d*) Heat may be lowered after pastry has set.

5. Proportions:

   (*a*) Suet: $\frac{1}{4}$–$\frac{1}{2}$ fat to flour.

   250 ml water to 500 g flour (approximately).

   4 level teaspoonfuls baking powder to 500 g flour (or S.R. flour).

   2 level teaspoonfuls salt to 500 g flour.

(*b*) Shortcrust:

> $\frac{1}{2}$ fat to flour.
>
> 150 ml water to 500 g flour (approximately).
>
> 2 level teaspoonfuls salt to 500 g flour.

(*c*) Rough puff and flaky:

> $\frac{2}{3}$–$\frac{3}{4}$ fat to flour.
>
> 250 ml water to 500 g flour.
>
> $\frac{1}{2}$ teaspoonful lemon juice to 500 g flour.
>
> 2 level teaspoonfuls salt to 500 g flour.

Rules for pastry making

1. Keep everything cool.
2. Use correct proportions.
   Note: '100 g pastry'
   means 100 g flour + fat,
   e.g. 100 g shortcrust =
   100 g flour + 50 g fat.
3. Right amount of water.
4. Little flour for rolling out.
5. Introduce as much air as possible.
6. Handle pastry lightly.
7. Leave to relax and cool before baking.
8. Correct oven temperature.

Notes on making

Suet crust

1. Flour, suet, baking powder, salt mixed.
2. Water added (elastic dough).
3. Rolled out (about $\frac{1}{2}$ cm thick).
4. Cooking: Steamed, boiled, baked.
5. Uses: Meat and fruit puddings, sweet or savoury roly-poly.

Short crust

1. Flour and salt sieved.
2. Fat rubbed into flour.
3. Water added (dough firm but not hard).
4. Kneaded lightly on board.
5. Rolled out (musn't be turned over).
6. Baked: Electric 425°F, 220°C, Gas Mark 7 until set. Reduced to 375°F, 190°C, Gas Mark 5 until cooked.
7. Uses: Pies, pastries, tarts, apple balls.
8. Variations:
   Cheese — $\frac{1}{2}$ to equal grated cheese to flour. Egg yolk may be used in mixing.
   (*a*) Used for savoury flans, cheese straws, etc.
   (*b*) Oven electric 325°F–350°F, 170°C–180°C, Gas Mark 3–4.

Biscuit crust — 25–50 g castor sugar to 500 g flour. Egg yolk may be used in mixing.
(*a*) Used for sweet flans.
(*b*) Oven electric 375°F, 190°C, Gas Mark 5.

Rough puff
1. Flour and salt sieved.
2. Even-sized small pieces of fat stirred into flour.
3. Water and lemon juice added (soft dough but not sticky).
4. Shaped into rectangle on board.
5. Rolled into long strip.
6. (*a*) Folded into three
   (*b*) Edges sealed.
   (*c*) Half turn to right ⎱ five times
   (*d*) Rolled into long strip ⎰
7. Left to relax twenty minutes in cool place. (May be left to relax between rollings if time.)
8. Rolled for use (thickness depends on article made).
9. Baking: (*a*) Electric 450°F, 230°C, Gas Mark 8 until set.
          (*b*) Electric 375°F, 190°C, Gas Mark 5 until cooked.
10. Uses: Meat pies and pasties, sausage rolls, mince pies, Eccles cakes, etc.

Flaky pastry

1. Flour and salt sieved.
2. (*a*) Fats creamed together and cooled (if two kinds are used).
   (*b*) $\frac{1}{4}$ of fat sometimes rubbed into flour.
3. Water and lemon juice added (soft dough — not sticky).
4. Dough kneaded well on board.
5. Shaped into rectangle on board.
6. Rolled into long strip.
7. (*a*) $\frac{1}{3}$ of fat dotted over top $\frac{2}{3}$ of dough
   (*b*) Folded into three
   (*c*) Edges sealed ⎫ three times
   (*d*) half turn to right
   (*e*) Rolled into long strip
8. Rolled and folded twice more.
9. Left to relax twenty minutes (may be left to relax between rollings if time).
10. Rolled for use (thickness depends on article made).

11. Baking: (*a*) Electric 450°F, 230°C, Gas Mark 8 until set.
    (*b*) Electric 357°F, 190°C, Gas Mark 5 until cooked.
12. Uses: Meat pies and pasties, sausage rolls, mince pies, Eccles cakes etc.

Scones

1. Plain mixture usually made by rubbing-in method.
2. Proportion of fat to flour low.
3. Scone dough should be soft and elastic, so a high proportion of liquid is used (milk or milk and water).
4. A little egg may be used — too much makes scones heavy.

Types of scones

Plain, fruit, cheese, potato, treacle (drop scones made with batter).

Proportions

1. $\frac{1}{8}$–$\frac{1}{4}$ fat to flour (plain).
2. $\frac{1}{8}$ sugar to flour ($\frac{1}{8}$ fruit for fruit scones).
3. 150 ml liquid to 200 g flour.
4. Raising agent
   (*a*) 4 level teaspoonsful baking powder to 200 g flour, *or*
   (*b*) 1 level teaspoonful of bicarbonate of soda + 2 level teaspoonsfuls of cream of tartar, *or*
   (*c*) If using sour milk to mix:
       1 level teaspoonful of cream of tartar + 1 level teaspoonful of bicarbonate of soda.

Notes on making

1. Flour, baking powder, salt, sieved.
2. Fat rubbed into flour.
3. Add liquid all at once.
4. Mix with palette knife (soft elastic dough).
5. Knead lightly (finger tips).
6. Roll or press to 2 cm thick.
7. Cut out.
8. May be brushed with milk.
9. Put on greased baking sheet.

Baking

1. Hot oven, 450°F, 230°C, Gas Mark 8.
2. Near top of oven.
3. Small scones about ten minutes. Larger about fifteen minutes.

Biscuits

1. Usually classified according to method used, e.g. rubbing-in, creaming, melting, whisking.
2. Less liquid is added as a rule than for cake mixtures.
3. Baked slowly to give crisp, short biscuits.
4. Often pricked to prevent rising.
5. Usually no raising agent.
6. Storing: (*a*) In air tight tins.
   (*b*) Never with cakes (absorb moisture and become soft).
7. Rubbing-in — coconut or any flavour.
   Creaming — Shrewsbury, Easter.
   Melting — Ginger nuts, brandy snaps.
   Whisking — Sponge fingers.

Flavouring and colouring food

Herbs

Herbs are usually the green parts of plants. They may be used fresh or dried.

Bay leaves. Come from a kind of laurel tree.
   Used in (*a*) sauces, stews
   (*b*) custards and milk puddings.

Chives. Have mild onion flavour.
   Used in salads, soups, omelettes and as a garnish.

Garlic. Belongs to the onion family. Has a very strong flavour.
   The dried bulb is made up of sections called 'cloves'. The cloves are crushed with a knife and finely chopped.
   Used in savoury dishes.
   For salads, it is enough to rub the inside of the bowl with a garlic clove.

Mint. Used in mint sauce or jelly to serve with lamb. Also cooked with potatoes and peas.

Parsley. Used in salads, soups, stuffings, sauce and as a garnish.

Sage. Has a strong flavour.
   Used mainly in stuffing for pork or duck.

Thyme. Used in stuffing for veal, fish or chicken. May also be used in soups, stews, sauces, omelettes.

Spices

Allspice. Tastes of several spices. Sold whole or ground.
Used mainly in savoury dishes.
Must not be confused with 'Mixed spice'.

Cinnamon. The bark of a kind of laurel tree. Sold in little sticks or powdered. Used in cakes, biscuits. Also in sauces and chutneys.

Cloves. Dried unopened flower buds of a tropical tree.
Used in sweet and savoury dishes, e.g. apple pies, chutneys, soups, stews.

Curry powder. A mixture of many spices. Very hot to taste.
Used for curries, sauces, soups.

Ginger. Prepared from the underground stem of a tropical plant.
Sold as root ginger, preserved ginger and ground ginger.
Used according to the recipe in cakes, biscuits and pickles. Also as an accompaniment to melon (ground).

Mustard. Dried and ground seeds of mustard plants.
Used in sauces, chutneys, curries.
Also used as an accompaniment to nearly all meat, particularly beef.

Nutmeg. The kernel of the fruit of the nutmeg tree grown in the East and West Indies. Sold whole or ground.
Used grated or ground over custards, junkets and milk puddings.
Note: The outside husk of the nutmeg is removed, ground and sold separately as Mace. It is used for savoury sauces, soups and pickles.

Pepper. Made from ground peppercorns. May be black or white.
Used to season nearly any savoury dish, in cooking or as a table condiment.
Peppercorns: Used in pickles and in soups and in stews which are strained.
Cayenne pepper: Made from ground chillies. Used in sauces, pickles, curry powder and on savouries.
Paprika: Made from dried capsicums. Used in stews, e.g. goulash as well as sauces and gravies. Adds a red colour to food.

Essences

Almond. Extracted from the kernel of bitter almonds.
Used to flavour cakes, pudding and sweets.

Orange and lemon. Obtained from the outside skin of the fruit.
Used in cakes, etc.

Peppermint. Sold as oil of peppermint.
Used for sweets, icings, etc.

Vanilla. Extracted from vanilla pods.
The pods may be used whole, e.g. to flavour milk for milk puddings.
Usually the essence is used for cakes, puddings and icings.

Artificial or *synthetic* essences are made in practically any flavour.

Cochineal. Made from a particular insect which is dried and crushed.
Gives a red colour to icings and sweets, etc.
Most colour including the red cochineal colour are now synthetic.

Convenience foods

Some kinds

1. Canned meat, fish, fruit, vegetables, soup, etc.
2. Packet soups, sauces, stock cubes.
3. Dehydrated vegetables.
4. Frozen vegetables, fruit, cream cakes, fish, meat, etc.
5. Cake and pastry mixes, tart cases, flan cases, etc.
6. Quick creaming fats.
7. Bottled sauces, salad cream, pickles, etc.
8. Baby foods.

Convenience foods are not all new, e.g. custard powder, jellies, etc.

Advantages

1. Often easy to carry home and easy to store.
2. Better than poor cooking.
3. Saves time and effort.
4. More variety in meals.
5. No waste.
6. Unaffected by seasonal price fluctuation.
7. Available throughout the year.
8. Useful for emergencies, e.g. shortage of time, bad weather, unexpected guests and cases of sickness.
9. Valuable for people living alone, especially elderly people (individual portions useful).
10. Easier for handicapped people to prepare meals.
11. Useful where cooking facilities are limited, e.g. bed-sits, caravans, holiday cooking etc.

Disadvantages

1. Often expensive.
2. Temptation to use them always, instead of fresh foods.
3. Flavour not always as good as fresh food.

General notes

1. Buy carefully, e.g. refuse badly dented tins, broken packets, etc.
2. If contents 'don't seem right' when opened, don't use — e.g. damp or unpleasant smell.
3. Store exactly according to directions, e.g. frozen foods.
4. Use according to directions. Don't try to keep left-overs to use later if told not to.

Preservation

1. Food should be preserved when it is at its best.
2. Preserved food should be safe, nutritious and appetising.
3. Food is preserved to prevent decay.

Why food decays

1. *Action of enzymes*
    (a) Enzymes are present in all living matter — they are chemical substaces.
    (b) Enzymes cause over-ripeness, which leads to decay.
    (c) Heat stops the action of enzymes by destroying them.

2. *Yeasts*
    (a) Are present in the air and on the skins of fruit.
    (b) They are tiny single-celled plants which multiply by budding.
    (c) They grow quickly when warm and moist.
    (d) Yeasts cause jams, fruits, etc. to ferment.
    (e) Destroyed by high temperatures.
    (f) Remain dormant in low temperatures.

3. *Moulds*
    (a) Are present in the air. They settle on food and multiply.
    (b) They are tiny plants.
    (c) They grow quickly in warm moist conditions.
    (d) Growth is checked by cold dry storage, high temperatures and acetic acid.

4. *Bacteria*

(*a*) Present in the air.
(*b*) They are tiny plants — the smallest of all living things.
(*c*) They multiply very quickly with food, warmth and moisture.
(*d*) Growth is prevented by low temperature, acids and strong solutions of sugar and salt.
(*e*) They are destroyed by very high temperatures.
(*f*) Some bacteria produce toxins which make food poisonous.

Aims of preservation

1. To destroy the destructive organisms in food or prevent them from growing.
2. To prevent others reaching the food.

Methods

1. Heat — high temperatures for certain length of time.
2. Cold — Freezing
3. Drying — Water is removed } Also freeze-drying.
4. Adding — Sugar, salt, acid or other chemical preservatives.

Heat

1. Destroys yeasts, moulds, bacteria and enzymes.
2. The food must then be sealed in the containers to keep out air.
3. Methods of preservation using heat are: Bottling and Canning.

Bottling

1. Most fruits suitable.
2. Water or sugar syrup used.
3. Vegetables require a very high temperature — need a pressure cooker to make vegetables safe.

Notes on fruit bottling:

(*a*) Best fruit.
(*b*) Careful preparation.
(*c*) Perfect jars, new rubber bands (if used).
(*d*) Careful packing.
(*e*) Sterilise in oven, water bath or pressure cooker (special bottles).
(*f*) Bottles must be about 5 cm apart.
(*g*) Seal tested next day — if not sealed successfully, re-process at once or serve as stewed fruit.

Canning (usually done commercially)

1. Foods — meat, fish, vegetables, fruit, puddings etc.
2. Cans — sheet steel — lined can and lacquered.
3. The tins of food are sterilised at a very high temperature.
4. Only good quality food can be used.
5. Not much loss of vitamins.

Cold (Freezing)

1. Food frozen to prevent growth of organisms.
2. Organisms not destroyed. They can grow again after food is thawed.
    Directions for use on frozen food packets must be followed exactly.
3. Food is frozen commercially and in deep freeze cabinets at home.
4. Quick   (*a*) Very low temperature.
    freezing: (*b*) Small ice crystals.
                     (*c*) Food does not break up or lose its flavour.
                     (*d*) Food — meat, poultry, fish, soft fruit, vegetables, cream cakes, etc.
5. At home: (*a*) Follow directions exactly.
                     (*b*) Use best fruit etc.
                     (*c*) Use correct containers.
                     (*d*) Thaw and use correctly.
Freeze-dried foods:
                     (*a*) Keep well.
                     (*b*) Easy to carry and store.
                     (*c*) Useful if no fridge.
                     (*d*) Easy to prepare.

Drying

1. Moisture removed:
                     (*a*) Done commercially, e.g. milk, soup, potatoes, eggs, vegetables, fruit, etc. (meat and fish may also be dried).
                     (*b*) At home, e.g. herbs, apple rings.
                     (*c*) Need to be stored in airtight containers — dried foods spoil quickly if they get damp.

Chemical preservation

1. Sugar — Jam, marmalade etc.
2. Acid — Pickles, chutneys, etc.
3. Salt — Meat, fish, bacon (at home green beans).
4. Fruit preserving tablets, e.g. Campden tablets, sometimes used.

1. Fresh fruit, just ripe or under ripe.
    (*a*) Contains most pectin
        Pectin + fruit acid + sugar help jam to set.
    (*b*) Fruit low in pectin, e.g. strawberries, need pectin added from other fruits, e.g. lemon juice.
2. Fruit cooked with water.
    Note: Slow cooking before sugar is added. Fast cooking after sugar is added.
3. Warmed sugar added slowly.
4. Mixture stirred until sugar is dissolved.
5. Quick boiling until setting point is reached.
6. Tests for setting:
    (*a*) Cold plate.
    (*b*) Flake.
    (*c*) Temperature.
    (*d*) Weight.
7. Potting:
    (*a*) Clean warm jars.
    (*b*) Cooling jam a little before potting stops fruit rising to top.
8. Cover:
    (*a*) Waxed circles + cellophane cover.
    (*b*) Jam covered at once or covered when quite cold.
9. Labelling: Type of jam, date, etc.
10. Storing: Cool, dry, dark place.

Beverages

Main ones taken are tea, coffee, cocoa, chocolate, fruit and various proprietary ones.

1. Food value small unless made with milk (animal protein) or containing vitamin C.
2. Beverages help to increase liquid intake.
3. Some proprietary drinks are very nutritious and easily digested. Useful as 'nightcaps' for invalids and children.

Tea

1. Made from dried leaves of shrubs grown in China, India, Sri Lanka and Japan.
2. Most tea imported from India, China and Sri Lanka.
    (*a*) China tea has the most delicate flavour, most caffeine and least tannin.
    (*b*) India and Sri Lanka tea have more body, colour and tannin.

3. Caffeine stimulates. Tannin hardens protein and interferes with digestion.
4. Making tea:
   (a) Heat the pot.
   (b) Use boiling water (take pot to kettle).
   (c) Allow 1 teaspoonful tea to 250 ml water (or according to taste).
   (d) Allow to stand in a warm place (infusing) for about four minutes.
   (e) If left to stand too long tannin is extracted, tea tastes bitter.

Coffee

1. Coffee beans come from inside the stones of the fruit of an evergreen shrub grown in the tropics, e.g. Brazil.
2. Coffee beans are roasted, ground and packed in airtight containers.
3. Coffee may be bought as beans (to grind at home), as ground coffee, as 'instant' coffee or coffee essence.
4. There are several ways of making coffee, e.g. in a jug, saucepan, ordinary pot, filter type pot, percolator etc.

   In an ordinary coffee pot:
   (a) Heat the pot, stand it in a warm place.
   (b) Put coffee in the pot (1 tablespoon to 250 ml water).
   (c) Pour on boiling water.
   (d) Stand it in warm place for about ten minutes.
   (e) Strain — serve hot with or without hot milk.

Cocoa

1. Comes from a marrow-like fruit from a tree grown in the tropics, e.g. West Africa.
2. Seeds are taken out of the fruit, undergo several processes to produce cocoa powder.
3. Not as stimulating as tea and contains little tannin; therefore more suitable for children.
4. To make:
   (a) Use 1 teaspoonful cocoa to 250 ml milk (or milk and water).
   (b) Mix cocoa (and sugar to taste) with a little of the cold liquid.
   (c) Boil rest of liquid and pour on to cocoa (stir all the time).
   (d) Pour into pan and bring back to boil (cooks the starch).

Most people probably prefer the strength given by a heaped spoonful, but it is a matter of taste.

Putting things right

Sometimes things do go wrong, but if you understand why, you are not likely to make the same mistake next time.

Cakes

Sunk in the middle
1. Oven door opened too soon (or slammed).
2. Cake moved before set.
3. Cake taken out of oven too soon.
4. Oven too cool.
5. Too much liquid used.
6. Too much raising agent.
7. Wet fruit.
8. Over creaming of fat, sugar and eggs (likely if a mixer is used).

Fruit sunk to the bottom
1. Wet fruit used.
2. Mixture too slack.
3. Oven too cool.

Cake risen too high in the middle — badly cracked
1. Cooked in too hot an oven.
2. Cooked on too high a shelf.

Pastry

Short pastry — hard and tough
1. Over-kneading — heavy rolling — pastry turned over.
2. Too much flour used in rolling out.
3. Too much water added.
4. Pastry cooked too slowly.
5. Wrong blending of fats.

Rough puff and flaky — hard and tough
1. Too much water.
2. Not kept cool.
3. Too much flour used in rolling out.
4. Rolled too long.
5. Oven too cool.

Rough puff and flaky — unevenly risen
1. Fat unevenly distributed.
2. Uneven rolling and folding.

3. Edges not cut off before using.
4. Not allowed to relax between rollings or before baking.

Pastry shrinking when cooked
1. Stretched when rolled or shaped.
2. Not allowed to relax before baking (rough puff between rollings too).

Suet pastry — hard and tough
1. Not enough baking powder or liquid.
2. Cooked too quickly.
3. Baked instead of steamed.

Suet pastry — heavy and wet
1. Not enough baking powder.
2. Pastry got wet during cooking (by steam or water).

Bread

Dough heavy — doesn't rise much during first rising
Liquid too hot — killed yeast.

Dough heavy — doesn't rise much after proving
Too much heat during first rising.

Loaves or rolls wrinkled on top after baking
(*a*) Dough over proved.
(*b*) Oven not hot enough to start with.

Bread has sour taste
(*a*) Rising and proving too slow.
(*b*) Stale yeast.
(*c*) Too much yeast.

Sauces

Lumpy
Roux: 1. Fat too hot when flour added.
           2. Liquid and roux not mixed smoothly or enough.
           3. Liquid added too quickly.
Blended: 1. Liquid and powder (e.g. cornflour) not blended smoothly.

Raw flavour
1. Roux not cooked long enough.
2. Sauce not cooked long enough.

Lacking gloss
1. Not cooked long enough after liquid was added.

Too thin
1. Wrong proportion of ingredients.
2. Over and undercooking.

Egg custards

Curdling
1. Too hot milk added to egg.
2. Overheating.
   To correct: Strain into cool basin and whisk well.

Junket

Not set
1. Milk too hot when rennet is added.
2. Junket not put in a warm place to set.
3. Dish moved whilst setting.

Jam

Not set
Not enough pectin or acid in the fruit.
   To correct: Add 2 tablespoons lemon juice to 2 kg of fruit and reboil.

Fruit risen to top
Jam put in pots whilst too hot.

Mould on top
(*a*) Covered whilst still damp.
(*b*) Stored in damp place.
(*c*) Too little sugar.

Jam crystallises
(*a*) Not enough acid in fruit.
(*b*) Too much sugar used.
(*c*) Jam boiled too long or not long enough.

Bottling

Fruit rising to top
(*a*) Too much sugar in syrup.
(*b*) Loose packing.
(*c*) Temperature raised too quickly.

Moulds forming
(*a*) Bottles not heated enough.   (*c*) Jars not covered with liquid.
(*b*) Heating at too low a temperature.(*d*) Leak in the seal.

Frying

Too greasy
(*a*) Fat not hot enough.
(*b*) Food not drained.

Black specks on food
Fat not strained after previous frying.

Rissoles etc. burst
(*a*) Coating not put on evenly.
(*b*) Fat not hot enough.

Food raw inside
Fat too hot so that outside looks brown before inside cooked.

Food changes

Changes in food occur when it is stored, prepared and cooked.

Storage

1. Perishable foods deteriorate quickly if they are left in a larder or kitchen too long, particularly in warm kitchens. The spoilage is caused by the invasion of yeasts, moulds, bacteria, by enzymes in the food and other chemical processes. Perishable foods should be kept in a refrigerator, freezer or cold larder but deterioration will still occur if the food is kept too long.
2. Many foods are spoilt if water or dampness is present. Flour, cereals, pulses, spices, dehydrated foods and packeted foods must all be kept dry. Jars with well-fitting lids are better than packets. Jam will go mouldy if it is kept in a damp place.
3. Other changes which occur during storage include the staling of bread. Fats and fat foods spoil because the fat goes rancid.
4. Some foods pick up the odours of other foods. Most foods are better stored wrapped.
5. Vitamin C in vegetables is lost when they are stored. By the end of the winter, potatoes which have been stored contain very little vitamin C. Where possible refrigeration helps to prevent loss.

Preparation and cooking

In the preparation and cooking of food two kinds of changes can occur, physical and chemical.

(a) Physical changes — include the setting of jellies and the making of salad cream when oil and vinegar are shaken together.

(b) Chemical changes — include the gelatinisation of starch, coagulation of eggs, coagulation and colour-change when meat is cooked and the conversion of starch to dextrin when bread is toasted.

Chemical changes are also due to:

(a) Osmosis, e.g. when prunes are soaked in water they swell because water molecules have passed through the skin.

(b) Diffusion — when molecules move from a region of high concentration to a region of lower concentration.

Solutions occur when substances dissolve in liquids, e.g. water soluble vitamins and minerals dissolve in the cooking water. Sugars also form solutions with water.

If water is mixed with large molecules, e.g. of starch or protein a colloidal solution is formed, e.g. blancmange, jelly, mayonnaise.

Flavour, colour and texture of food

1. Appetising food stimulates the digestive juices and aids good digestion.
2. People appreciate food through the senses of sight, smell, taste and feeling.
3. The sensory properties of food include the taste, smell, appearance, texture and temperature.

The flavour of food

1. There are two kinds of flavour, volatile and non-volatile. The taste organs are concerned with the non-volatile components of food which are sweetness, sourness, bitterness and saltiness.
2. True flavour comes from the stimulation of the olfactory epithelium in the nasal cavity by volatile flavours which are recognised as odours.
3. Volatile substances are substances which vaporise when exposed to air. What is referred to as the taste of food is a combination of the sensation of the taste buds and the stimulation of the olfactory hairs in the upper nasal cavity.
4. Temperatures affect the sense of taste. Sweet drinks appear sweeter when hot than cold. A lemon drink seems more sour when it is hot than when it is cold.
5. Substances used to flavour food include sugar, salt, acids, condiment and spices.
6. The flavour of food can be intensified by the use of mono-sodium glutamate (MSG), which is the salt of glutamic acid.

7. Commercial food flavours may be extracted from food (expensive) or made from synthetic flavours (cheaper). A mixture of natural and synthetic flavours are sometimes used. Synthetic flavours are subject to the food laws.
8. Different methods of cooking produce different flavours, e.g. boiled and roast potatoes.
9. In cooking the blending of flavours is important. For instance marmalade is a blend of sweetness and bitterness.

Colour of food

Some people will like or dislike food depending on its colour. Children like brighter coloured food than adults do. Fruit and vegetables are useful to add colour to meals as well as for their nutritional value. The main colours found in fruit and vegetables include the following:

Chlorophyll: Green, in green leafy vegetables.

Carotenoids: Yellow to red, in carrots, peaches, tomatoes, apricots.

Flavenoids: (*a*) Anthocyonins: Red to violet, in plums, strawberries and some other berry fruits.

(*b*) Flavones: Yellow to white, in apples, onions, cauliflower.

To prevent fruit and vegetables going brown:

1. Destroy enzymes — blanch (put into very hot water).
2. Add acid — e.g. put into water with lemon juice.
3. Keep out of air — store in plain cold water or salt water.
4. Add vitamin C or sodium metabisulphite — dissolve these in water and add to food.

Notes

1. Sodium bicarbonate is sometimes added to greens to keep them a bright colour but it destroys the vitamin C. If the rest of the diet is likely to be lacking in vitamin C it is better not to add sodium bicarbonate to the greens.
2. The food laws allow some synthetic colours to be added to food.
3. Cooking affects the colour of food, e.g. bread browns when toasted. Different methods of cooking produce articles of a different colour, e.g. baked and steamed jam roly-poly. Colour may be lost, e.g. greens (see note 1 above).

Texture of food

Foods feel different when in the mouth, e.g. they may feel hard, soft, crispy, creamy, tough, gritty, watery etc. As regards texture, foods fit into two main types.

1. Foods which still contain the basic structure of the plant or animal from which the food comes, e.g. potatoes, meat, raw whole fruit and vegetables.
2. Foods which have lost all or some of their plant or animal structure, e.g. some bread, meat pastes.

Notes

When planning meals it is important to include food of different textures, e.g. shepherd's pie for first course should not normally be followed by rice pudding for second course.

It is important for children to have some crisp and chewy foods so that they get into the habit of biting and chewing and their food can be properly digested. Biting and chewing also helps in the development of jaws and teeth.

Food additives

Food additives may be used for various reasons, e.g.
   (*a*) To prevent food spoilage.
   (*b*) To lengthen the time the food will keep in good condition.
   (*c*) To improve the texture, flavour or appearance of the food.

Preventing food spoilage

(*a*) Preservatives may be added to foods such as meat and meat products, fish and fish products, fruit, jam, cheese, bread and soft drinks.
(*b*) Permitted preservatives include sodium nitrate, sulphur dioxide, benzoin acid to prevent the growth of micro-organisms.
(*c*) Mineral oils such as liquid paraffin are only allowed in eggs, cheese, dried fruits, sugar confectionary and chewing compounds.
   Only the permitted amounts can be used.
(*d*) To prevent fats turning rancid certain antioxidants may be added, e.g. propyl, dodecyl and acetyl.

To improve texture, colour and flavour

(*a*) Emulsifiers may be added to improve texture as in margarine to obtain a uniform dispersion of water and fat.
(*b*) Stabilisers may be added to prevent uniform dispersions separating out as in instant deserts.

(*c*) Manufacturers believe that people like the colour of food to match its flavour and like the colour of food to be the colour they think it ought to be. Therefore the manufacturers add permitted colourings and flavourings to food. Colour may be lost in manufacture and permitted colour may be added to correct this.

The law and food

The Food and Drugs Act 1955

The most important provisions of this Act include:
1. It is an offence to sell food which is not of the nature, substance or quality demanded.
2. Labels and advertising must not describe a food falsely or mislead as to the nature, substance or quality of the food.
3. The addition or subtraction of any substance from food which would make it injurious to health is forbidden.
4. The selling of unsound food is an offence.

The Labelling of Food Regulations 1970

The following are some of the regulations included in this Act.
1. Most packaged foods must bear:
   (*a*) A common or usual name or an appropriate designation of the food.
   (*b*) A list of ingredients in descending order by weight.
2. The name and address of the packer or labeller or somebody resident in the United Kingdom who is responsible for the food must be shown.
3. Claims on the label or in advertising must be valid. E.g. The food is useful for diabetics, slimmers, is a good source of protein, energy etc.
4. Claims of vitamin or mineral content can only be made for the following:
   Vitamin A, thiamin, riboflavin, nicotinic acid, vitamin C, vitamin D, iron, calcium and iodine.

Other food regulations include:

1. *The Sausage and Other Meat Product Regulations 1967* (as amended) says:
   (*a*) A pork sausage must contain 65% meat.
   (*b*) A beef sausage must contain 50% meat.

2. *The Bread and Flour Regulations 1963* (as amended)
   (*a*) The use of colouring matter is restricted.
   (*b*) The permitted bleaching and improving agents must be listed.
   (*c*) Minimum nutrients levels for flour are prescribed.
   (*d*) The amount of chalk which must be added to all flour except self-raising, wholemeal and wheat malt flour is laid down.

3. *The Margarine Regulations 1967* include the following:
   (*a*) All margarine for retail sale must be fortified with vitamins A and D.
   (*b*) The label must contain this information.

Hygiene

The kitchen

Floors

1. Should have smooth surface — cracks, holes, rough surfaces collect dirt and germs.
2. Be easily cleaned.
3. Vinyl, good lino, well fitted tiles, all suitable.

Walls

1. Should be smooth and washable.
2. Rounded corners make cleaning easier.
3. Tiles, gloss paint and vinyl all easily cleaned.

Ceilings

1. Should be no loose bits to fall into food.
2. Must be absorbent — collected moisture can fall onto food and contaminate it.

Non-washable distemper useful but needs to be re-done about every six months.

Lighting

Very important for cleanliness:
   (*a*) So that dirt can be noticed in corners, etc.
   (*b*) Because insects like dark corners.

Ventilation

1. Bacteria multiply very quickly in warm places.
2. Need a current of air to cool kitchen and take out steam and fumes.
   (a) Kitchen window open a little whilst cooking.
   (b) Extractor fans and cooker hoods useful.

Equipment

All kitchen equipment should be:
   (a) Easy to clean.
   (b) Easy to dismantle and put together again (otherwise it won't get cleaned often).
   (c) Bought with a view to easy and complete cleaning.
   (d) Thrown away when difficult to clean, chipped, etc.

Sinks

1. Old rough sinks collect germs — regular and efficient cleaning vital for these, e.g. use of bleach etc.
2. Double sinks are best if possible.
3. Use separate bowl for washing up.

Cupboards, shelves, tables

1. Should have hard smooth surfaces, e.g. metal, formica, or several coats of gloss paint.
2. Fewer ledges, corners and joins the better.
3. Floor standing equipment must be easy to pull out for cleaning under and behind.

Cleaning

1. Regular cleaning is very important and everything should be done to make this as easy and efficient as possible.
2. Danger spots:
   (a) Food work tops only wiped. Need thorough daily wash.
   (b) Slots in sliding doors on cupboards.
   (c) Ledges on top of half-tiled walls.
   (d) Cupboard and pipes under sink.
   (e) Cutlery drawer.
   (f) Sink outlets and outside drain.
3. Pedal bins and dustbins need hot water scrubs and disinfecting.
4. Wrap rubbish in paper — empty pedal bins often.
5. Don't use teatowels for wiping up spills.

Pests — spread disease:

1. Don't leave scraps of food about anywhere.
2. Put food away as soon as possible.
3. Repair holes in walls, floors, etc.
4. Keep drains in good repair.
5. Only put small pieces of food out for birds, large pieces attract rats.
6. Signs of rats and mice are — holes, droppings, greasy marks on walls, teeth marks on food.
7. Try trap for mice. Use dangerous killers with special care. Contact Public Health Department for rats.
8. Insect killers — Use according to directions, make sure they don't get on food.

Food

Food may be infected by:
1. People — bacteria from nose, throat, cuts, bowels, sores.
2. Animals — domestic, rats, mice, flies, etc.
3. Other infected food or water.
4. Dirt, dust, etc.

A. *Buying*

1. Clean shop, clean assistants, clean bag, clean wrappings.
2. Don't buy cooked meat from shop where same assistant handles raw and cooked meat.
3. Don't buy frozen food where fridges are overflowing or food is left around shop for some time before being put in fridge.
4. Look for date stamps.
5. Mind where you put shopping bag.
6. Be clean yourself — no sneezing, breathing on food, touching it or taking dogs into shops.
7. Contact Public Health department if premises, assistants, food etc. seem unhygienic.

B. *Storing and keeping*

1. Put all perishables straight into a clean fridge.
2. Keep all food, cool, clean, covered.
3. Follow directions on packets exactly regarding keeping.
4. Fridge — Keep clean, pack loosely, only put fresh food in. Check contents regularly.
5. Always use clean containers and lids.

6. Use up perishable foods quickly.
7. Never put pet food near human food — don't put in fridge, can contaminate human food.
8. Check larder often — keep spotless.
9. Useful storage items — milk and butter coolers, cooling cabinets, polythene canisters and bags, nylon net covers.

C. *Preparing and serving food*

1. Wash hands before handling food. Extra care if food is ready to eat, e.g. cooked meats.
2. Wash hands, chopping board and knife after chopping raw meat.
3. Wash hands after using toilet — *very* important.
4. Keep hands and nails very clean.
5. Clean aprons, hair tied back.
6. Never smoke while preparing food.
7. Don't put spoon used for testing back into the food.
8. A person with a cold (if there is nobody else to get food ready) must:
    (*a*) Choose foods which need little preparing.
    (*b*) Use paper handkerchiefs (burn or put down lavatory).
    (*c*) Wash hands after using handkerchief.
    (*d*) Never cough or sneeze into hand.
9. Cuts, scratches etc. must be kept covered with waterproof dressing.
10. Handle food as little as possible.
11. Serve hot foods as soon as they are ready.
12. Make sure everybody who touches food keeps food hygiene rules too.
13. Preparing food in advance:
    (*a*) Cool food quickly — protect food whilst cooling.
    (*b*) Put cool food in fridge or cold larder.
    (*c*) Don't part-cook meat the day before — may be dangerous.
    (*d*) Don't prepare party food too far in advance unless you have a cold store (e.g. fridge) large enough.
14. Left-   (*a*) Try not to have any.
    overs: (*b*) Don't leave oddments in fridge too long.
             (*c*) Safer not to keep gravy, custard, jellies, even in the fridge (bacteria multiply very quickly in these foods).
15. Re-heated foods (left-overs or bought pies etc.)
    (*a*) Making hot for a few minutes or just warming multiplies germs.
    (*b*) Recommended oven time is 20 min. at Mark 7 (Electric 425°F, 220°C) — after the oven is hot. On top of the cooker — bring to boil and cook for at least 15 minutes.

D. *Most easily infected foods*

1. (*a*) All cooked meat, meat dishes and meat products.
   (*b*) Gravy, soups and sauces.
   (*c*) Underdone pork is very dangerous.
   (*d*) Children must never be allowed to eat raw meat, especially pork sausages.
2. Any food containing gelatine, e.g. jellies, etc.
3. Custard, ice-cream, synthetic cream, cream cakes.
4. Shell fish.
5. Watercress and salad foods — wash carefully.
6. Eggs, especially duck eggs. Eggs shouldn't be eaten underdone. Duck eggs should be boiled for at least ten minutes.
7. Sandwiches — meat, fish, egg, pastes.

E. *General notes*

1. Dried foods should be eaten as soon as possible after they have been made up.
2. Canned foods — don't use them if they don't smell or look good. Wipe tops before opening. Take care with home bottled foods too.
3. Animal food — raw pet food is always a source of danger to humans. Use separate knives, plates, etc. for preparing and wash them separately afterwards.
4. Dangerous times — food poisoning most likely to occur:
   (*a*) In summer months.
   (*b*) At Christmas and party times.
   (*c*) When somebody in the family has sore throat, intestinal illness, etc. They should have their own dishes, cutlery etc. which should be washed separately.
5. Babies' food — extra care needed especially when babies are tiny. Doctors, clinics, midwives, health visitors will give advice.

F. *Washing up*

1. Scrape and rinse plates, pans, etc. before washing up.
2. Use hot water and some kind of washing-up liquid.
3. Change water when dirty.
4. Rinse under hot water and put to drain rather than dry on tea towels.
5. Don't let people dry hands on tea towels.
6. Give cloths, nylon scourers etc. a regular boil.
7. Wear gloves if you have cuts etc.
8. Handling dry crockery and cutlery — try not to put hands in cups, hold knife blades, etc.

Kitchen equipment (see also section on hygiene)

Planning

Kitchen should be safe, convenient to work in, easy to clean and pleasant.

1. Types: (a) Working kitchen.
   (b) Working kitchen and dining room.
   (c) Working kitchen and living room.
2. Large equipment should be arranged for easy working sequence.
3. Working surfaces, sinks etc. should be the correct height to avoid strain.
4. Tools, utensils etc. should be stored near to where they are usually used.

Large equipment — Points to consider

1. *Cookers*

(a) Kind of fuel, e.g. electric, gas, solid fuel.
(b) How much money can be afforded.
(c) Size to fit kitchen, for number of people. (e.g. oven size, number of hot plates.)
(d) Space for heating plates, storing cooking utensils.
(e) Will saucepans balance, especially small ones?
(f) Position of grill.
(g) Easy to clean, self-cleaning etc.
(h) Is it strongly made — any sharp edges?

Using: (a) Use safely and economically.
   (b) Clean regularly.
   (c) Make full use of any modern devices, e.g. automatic lighting, automatic timing etc.

2. *Sinks*

(a) Price and size.
(b) Material, e.g. stainless steel, porcelain, plastics, etc.
(c) Double sinks, draining board both sides, left hand draining board.
Using: (a) Clean regularly — use correct cleaner.
   (b) Keep outlets clean.
   (c) Avoid blocking.

3. *Refrigerators*

(a) Price.

(*b*) Type — Absorption — silent. Compression cheaper to run.

(*c*) Size — To fit kitchen space.
Of family — 0.028 cu metre space for each person.
Of freezing compartment. (Unless you have a freezer, which should be as large as possible).

(*d*) Good finish to interior— well fitting shelves— well fitting door. Easy and accessible control.

Using: (*a*) Store food according to instructions.
(*b*) Don't pack too tightly.
(*c*) Clean regularly.
(*d*) Keep tidy — check contents regularly.
(*e*) Cool food before putting in.
(*f*) Don't leave door open unnecessarily.
(*g*) Cover food and use smallest containers.

4. *Freezers*

(*a*) Freezers may be free standing, upright or chest types or combined with a refrigerator.

(*b*) When buying a freezer consider price, the space you have to put it and the size you require. 'Extras' usually add to the price but a warning bell or light which tells you if the temperature has risen above a safe level is worth the extra money.

(*c*) Ask about servicing when buying.

(*d*) If possible take out an insurance policy to cover loss of food in the case of power failure.

Using: (*a*) Have the freezer properly installed.
(*b*) Read the instruction book (keep the book in a safe place).
(*c*) If the freezer is moved make sure it stands level when put back in place.
(*d*) Store food according to the instructions.
(*e*) Keep the freezer and food containers clean.
(*f*) Pack and label food carefully.
(*g*) Never refreeze food which has been thawed (dangerous bacteria can multiply).
(*h*) Don't open the lid or door more often than necessary and never leave the door or lid open.
(*i*) Put frozen food in as soon as possible (gloves useful if you are packing a large amount).
(*j*) Cool food quickly until it is quite cold before freezing it.

Advantages of home-freezers

(*a*) Bulk buying of some foods to save money, e.g. fruit, vegetables, carcases of meat.

(*b*) Storing surplus garden produce.

(*c*) Storing foods bought cheaply in season to use out of season, e.g. fruit, vegetables.

(*d*) For emergency supplies, e.g. in case of illness, food shortages, etc.

(*e*) Storing commercially frozen foods.

(*f*) Saving time in cooking — cook large quantities and freeze.

(*g*) Saving time in shopping — buy extra and store in freezer.

(*h*) Adds variety to meals.

(*i*) Special occasion food can be prepared and stored in advance.

(*j*) Storing items to use for cooking later, e.g. pastry, cake mixes, doughs, etc.

(*k*) Makes it possible for old people, invalids, handicapped people, people who go out to work, people who can't or don't like cooking to have a better diet.

5. *Dishwashers*

Many types, may open at top or front. Sizes for six, eight, twelve place settings. May be semi-portable or permanently installed. Time savers especially if the family is large or much entertaining is done.

Use and care includes following manufacturer's instructions, regular maintenance, using correct detergent, careful loading, economical use.

6. *Waste-disposal unit*

Hygienic and convenient way of getting rid of food waste. A large outlet is made in the centre of the sink and the waste-disposal unit is fitted underneath. Rubbish is put in, cold water turned on and the electric current operates the cutters which churn waste into small pieces. Waste-disposal units will deal with food scraps, such as peelings, pieces of bone, fat etc. Tins and rags should not be put into the unit. Important to read instructions carefully and exercise care in use.

7. *Extractor fans*

Essential in a kitchen but fairly expensive. Useful to clear the room of greasy fumes and hot air and therefore helpful for rest of house. An extractor fan can be fitted into a window pane or into an outside wall (extra expense). Extractor fans should be cleaned regularly to ensure efficient working. Dirt and dust get trapped in the fan and usually the fan unit can be removed for cleaning purposes.

Cookery hoods with a fitted extractor fan are very useful for removing fumes etc. from the cooker area before they can contaminate the rest of the air. Both extractor fans and cooker hoods help to keep a kitchen clean.

Work surfaces

Materials used for kitchen work surfaces include wood, stainless steel, vitreous enamel, plastic laminates, e.g. Formica, and pseudo-plastic laminates, e.g. Fablon.

Stainless steel. Used for draining boards — expensive.

Wood. Tables and older types of draining boards (avoid cutting, staining, burning with hot pans, cleanliness important).

Vitreous enamel. Used for some draining boards, some table tops (avoid scratching, clean and dry after use).

Plastic laminates. Many advantages, e.g. reasonably priced, attractive, easily fixed to flat surfaces, practically heat and stain resistant, strong and easy to clean.

For working surfaces a good quality plastic is required. Very hot pans should not be put on them, protect with wooden triangle or board.

Should not chop on them, use chopping board.

Cleanliness important but don't use harsh scourers.

Pseudo-plastic laminates. Attractive, easily wiped clean, but easily stained, damaged by knives, heat etc.

Small equipment — Points to consider

1. *Saucepans*

Usually made of aluminium, stainless steel, copper, vitreous enamel.

Aluminium. Advantages – Heats quickly, heavy quality lasts for years. Disadvantages — Become discoloured, cheap ones may lose shape. Cast aluminium expensive. Can become pitted.

Stainless steel. Advantages — Hard wearing and attractive, easily cleaned, rust resistant.
Disadvantages — Not a good conductor of heat, better if copper bottomed but expensive. Plain stainless steel becomes brown with high temperatures.

Copper. Advantages — Very good conductor of heat, food less likely to burn, hard wearing.

Disadvantages — Heavy, expensive, tarnishes easily, needs relining after a few years.

Vitreous enamel. Advantages — Strong, attractive.
Disadvantages — can chip and stain, slow to heat up.

Non-stick pans. Advantages — Good for milk and frying. Best ones remain 'non-stick' and can be used for 'dry' frying.
Disadvantages — Best ones expensive, others may need re-coating after a time.

Over-heating spoils surface of some of these pans (as can hard scouring).

Notes

1. Buy type to suit cooker, e.g. electric cookers and solid fuel cookers need flat-bottomed, ground based, fairly heavy pans.
2. Size important, e.g. for number in family, elderly people living alone.
3. Pan handles and lid knobs should remain cool. Lids should fit well but not too tightly.
4. Should be easy to clean, e.g. rounded where sides meet bottom.
5. Should balance well when held. Very large saucepans should have two handles.

2. *Kettles*

(*a*) One large and one small useful.
(*b*) Electric — should switch itself off.
(*c*) It should not be possible for steam to touch the hand when kettle is held.

3. *Frying pans*

(*a*) One large and one small useful. Also an omelette pan.
(*b*) Metal as for saucepans.
(*c*) Some people like a lid.
(*d*) Handle which doesn't get too hot and is not too long.
(*e*) Electric ones with various uses are available.

4. *Baking tins*

(*a*) Meat, cakes, bread, baking sheets etc.
(*b*) Aluminium, non-rusting tin, non-stick.
(*c*) Should have no sharp edges, rolled edges safer.
(*d*) Loose bottomed cake tins useful. Also bun tins of various sizes.

5. *Casseroles*

(*a*) Oven-proof glass, flame-proof (may be used on hot plates), earthenware, vitreous enamel.
(*b*) Should be safe to hold — lip easy to grip.
(*c*) Good for 'oven to table' use.

6. *Cutlery*

(*a*) Knives — Bread saw, large chopping knife (18–20 cm blade). Vegetable knife (8–10 cm blade). Palette knives (large and small). Vegetable peeler (left handed if necessary). All should be best quality, sharp and well balanced.
(*b*) Forks — Most types useful but a long-handled one also necessary.
(*c*) Spoons — Table, dessert, tea, wooden. Strainer type also useful. British Standard spoons and cups help accurate measuring.
(*d*) Scissors — chromium or stainless steel. Saw-edged blades useful. Handles should be rounded to prevent cutting into fingers.

7. *Whisks*

(*a*) Rotary, coiled, flat, balloon. One of each if possible.

8. *Graters*

(*a*) Tinned, plastic, stainless steel.
Stainless steel best but expensive.
Box shaped with different sized teeth most useful.
(*b*) Mouli-grater useful for cheese etc.

9. *Mincer*

(*a*) Easy to clean.
(*b*) Easy to use — must fix firmly to table etc.
(*c*) Large enough for requirements.
(*d*) Able to mince food fine, medium and coarse.

10. *Sieve*

(*a*) One each of nylon and rustless wire.
(*b*) Not too small.
(*c*) Easy to clean.
(*d*) Large strainers, wire and nylon, suit some people better.

11. *Rolling pin*

(*a*) Wood, porcelain, glass.
(*b*) Long are best.

12. *Boards*

(*a*) Pastry boards if no formica surface available.
(*b*) Chopping board — large enough.

13. *Electric food mixers*

(*a*) Before buying consider how much you are likely to use it and what you want it to do.
(*b*) There is a very large range and models vary from simple hand held types to larger models with many attachments, e.g. liquidiser or blender goblet, grater, mincer, slicer, shredder, juice extractor, juice separator, etc.
(*c*) Look at several types and makes before you buy. Size can be a problem if you haven't a convenient space for it in the kitchen.
(*d*) Read the instructions carefully before using the mixer and keep the intructions in a safe place.
(*e*) It is important to keep the mixer and attachments very clean and to dry them carefully.
(*f*) Never rinse mixers under the tap whilst the mixer is plugged in to the electric point.

14. *Tea- and coffee-makers*

(*a*) Before buying, decide how much you are likely to use them.
(*b*) Coffee-makers may be heated in various ways, e.g. electricity, gas, or methylated burner.
(*c*) Coffee-makers are made from a variety of substances, e.g. anodised aluminium, glazed earthenware, glass, pottery, etc.
(*d*) Both tea and coffee makers must be washed, rinsed and dried after use.

15. *Various*

(*a*) Colander — stainless steel if possible.
(*b*) Can opener — must work! Wall types useful.
(*c*) Corkscrew.
(*d*) Cutters — strong — plastic breaks, tin rusts, stainless steel available.
(*e*) Fish slice.
(*f*) Flour dredger — top large enough for easy filling. Plastic and metal.

(*g*) Lemon squeezer — glass, aluminium.
(*h*) Refuse bin — easy to clean and use.
(*i*) Scales.
(*j*) Storage jars — easy to hold and clean, convenient sizes.
(*k*) Jugs of various sizes, glass, plastic etc.
(*l*) Forcing bag and tubes.

16. *Bowls and basins*

(*a*) Convenient sizes, easy to stack.
(*b*) Glass, plastic, earthenware, stainless steel, nylon.

17. *Cloths*

(*a*) Paper cloths — many uses, disposable.
(*b*) Others — hand, tea, oven, floor, dish.

Notes

(*a*) Buy necessary items first.
(*b*) Buy safest and best.
(*c*) Use carefully — keep very clean.

Plastic ware

Many articles used in the kitchen which used to be made of wood, metal or china are now made of plastics. The following are some examples.

1. *Thermoplastic plastics*

Include polythene, polystyrene, perspex, polyvinyl chloride (PVC) and nylon. Moulded thermoplastics, when reheated will soften and melt.
 Some thermoplastics are flexible when quite thin, e.g. polythene.

2. *Thermosetting plastics*

Include melamine, laminated plastic, bakelite and polyurethane. When reheated at high temperatures they will break down and char.

Melamine. Is light in colour and therefore can be coloured. Used for tea and dinner sets, melamine may be warmed in ovens up to a temperature of 100°C (200°F). It must not be exposed to naked flame or radiant hot plates.

Polythene. May be low density, which is soft, flexible and light, or high density, which is hard, rigid and heavy. Solid polythene feels waxy. Polythene can be made into a flexible waterproof film and is used for bags and wrappings. Bags for vegetables have holes in them to prevent vegetables rotting.

(All polythene bags should be kept away from children).

Solid polythene is made into bowls, buckets, detergent bottles, rubbish bins etc.

Polystyrene. May be clear, opaque or expanded. Clear polystyrene — used for measuring jugs, egg cups, containers, tumblers etc.

Opaque polystyrene — toughened with synthetic rubber and used for lining refrigerators.

Expanded polystyrene — a good insulator and feels warm to the touch. Used for ceiling tiles, throw-away cups and packaging.

Polyvinyl Chloride (PVC). PVC is a plastic of the vinyl group. Uses in the kitchen include adhesive plastic film which is used for table tops, shelves and other surfaces, washable floor tiles, table cloths, stool-covers, aprons.

In its hard form PVC may be used for refrigerator linings.

Perspex is an acrylic plastic. Has a glass like transparency, is hard and tough. Used for sinks, basins, baths.

Nylon. Several kinds (all polyamides). May be in the form of fibre, filaments or solid plastic. It is strong, rot proof, unaffected by mildew and moths, resistant to dirt, absorbs very little moisture (hydrophobic), resistant to alkalis and weak acids.

Uses in the kitchen include:

(*a*) Nylon fibre — curtains, rugs, carpet.

(*b*) Nylon filaments — brushes, brooms, cords.

(*c*) Solid nylon — gears and bearings of food mixers and beaters. (Need no oiling and quiet in use). Also used for curtain runners.

(*d*) Nylon basins can be used for steaming.

(*e*) Nylon scourers (don't scratch).

Laminated plastics. Made into sheets. Used for surfacing tables, cupboards, etc.

Caring for plastics

Wash and dry after use. Do not use harsh scourers or abrasive powders.

Keep away from direct heat and high temperatures. Generally speaking the thermoplastic plastics will melt and the thermosetting plastics will break and char.

Follow any directions given by manufacturers.

Glass ware

1. Glass is incombustible, inorganic, not hygroscopic, non-absorbent, chemically quite stable. Glass will not rust or rot, is resistant to staining, does not hold odours and flavours and is resistant to chemicals. Glass is thermoplastic. It can be melted and reshaped over and over again.

2. Thermal expansion is an important factor in the resistance of glass to stresses of heat, shock and alternating heat and cooling.

    The alkali content is very important in thermal expansion. Sodium and potassium oxide increase thermal expansion.

3. Thermal endurance is affected by thermal expansion, mechanical strength, the dimensions of the article and the rate at which heat is spread. Soft-working glass rods when dropped into cold water will withstand a shock of 112°C, whereas PYREX rods will withstand a shock of 325°C.

4. Thermal conductivity is decreased by high soda-potash and lead-oxide content. It is increased by high silicon and boric-oxide content.

5. Glass and hygiene — Cracked or chipped table ware and food containers are a health hazard because when the glass is broken the exposed area becomes absorbent. Germs are harboured and infection can be spread.

    Glass is homogenous and non-porous throughout and therefore will not harbour germs as can earthenware. Hospitals use opal glass ware because of its hygienic properties. Many homes also use this type of table ware.

6. Effects of heat on glass. Glass is a pour conductor of heat. If boiling water is poured into an ordinary glass container it will break. This is because the inside of the glass becomes hot and expands but the outside remains unchanged. (Jam jars are warmed in the oven before hot jam is poured into them but care still has to be taken).

    For glass to withstand wide changes of temperature it must have a low coefficient of linear expansion. This depends on the amount of silica in the glass. Pure fused silica can be used but borax is usually used for domestic glass.

    The addition of borax produces a glass which has a low expansion and is easy to melt and shape. This kind of glass is called borosilicate.

7. Flame-ware is a glass ceramic and is very tough. (Discovered by accident in 1957 when a photosensitive glass was heated several hundred degrees above the intended temperature.) The glass turned into a strong opaque material. Flame-ware was developed from this.

    The advantage of flame-ware is its exceptional resistance to shock. It can be:

(*a*) Taken straight out of the refrigerator and put into a hot oven.

(*b*) Used on top of the cooker as a saucepan or frying pan.

8. Choosing ovenproof glassware. Choose articles which can be used for more than one purpose.

Look for the guarantee.

Patterned articles. Find out if manufacturers will continue the pattern.

Check for balance, well fitting lids, ease of stacking, ease of carrying ('handles').

9. Care of glass — Treat it gently, store carefully, wash according to instructions, soak if badly stained, use for purpose it is intended. Use a plastic bowl (or mat in sink) when washing up. Generally better to wash glassware separately and only a few articles in the bowl at a time. Never use metal scourers or abrasive powders.

Vacuum-ware

Vacuum-ware is made in a variety of sizes and shapes with narrow or wide necks. Its uses include:

(*a*) Keeping food hot, e.g. drinks, soups, porridge, casseroles, stews (not safe to keep the baby's milk in for long periods).

(*b*) Keeping food cold, e.g. drinks, cold sweets.

(*c*) Keeping food crisp, e.g. salad vegetables.

Cooking time may be saved because the retention of heat continues the cooking process.

A vacuum flask consists of a double-walled glass vessel sealed at the neck. The flask is annealed to eliminate stress. A small hole is made and a glass tube is fused on the outer wall. A solution of silver nitrate is pumped in between the two walls of the flask so that the interior walls are coated. This coating prevents heat loss by radiation. Surplus liquid is sucked out from between the walls. The small tube is cut and sealed.

Every vessel is tested by being filled with boiling water, stoppered and left for twenty-four hours. The temperature of the water is tested and the vessel put in its outer casing.

Vacuum flasks prevent heat loss by:

(*a*) Conduction — double walls with a vacuum between and silvered interior walls prevents conduction of heat.

(*b*) Convection — no convection currents in a vacuum.

(*c*) Radiation — this is prevented by giving the inner wall a brightly polished surface and a bright surface on the outer wall. Any heat radiated from the inner wall is reflected back.

Kitchen accessories

Paper, Polythene and Foil. Paper towels — useful for hands, spills, draining fried foods etc.

Greaseproof paper useful for wrapping food, lining cake tins etc.

Polythene sheet and bags have many uses. Can be washed and used again. (If used for meat or fish safer to dispose of them after use.)

Foil sheet and foil containers used for wrapping food, covering food whilst cooking, lining cake tins etc. Can sometimes be re-used after careful washing.

Piping bags. May be made of nylon plastic or linen. Wash very well after use and store in clean place.

Muslin. Useful for straining soups and sauces etc. Wash well and dry after ue.

Thick flannel. Used to make jelly bags (for straining jellies). Wash and dry carefully after use and store in a dry place.

Kitchen safety

Electricity

1. Must have enough power points.
2. All equipment must be: (*a*) Properly earthed and wired.
                           (*b*) Checked regularly.
3. Never leave a child in the kitchen when electrical equipment is working, e.g. washing machines, driers, food mixers, irons.
4. Never fill an electric kettle from the tap whilst it is plugged into the socket, even if the switch is at 'off'.
   Short leads on kettles are safest.
5. Never wash hand food mixer beaters whilst still plugged into socket even if switch is at 'off'.
6. Don't stand on a wet floor when ironing.

Gas

1. Equipment must be correctly installed and regularly checked.
2. If a gas leak is suspected contact the Gas Board at once.
3. If meter runs out, turn all taps off.
4. Keep a check on pilot lights in case they blow out.
5. Make sure burners are alight before leaving them, e.g. automatic.
6. Have safety taps fitted to cookers if there are small children about.
7. Avoid draughts which may blow gas out.

Cooker

1. Should be in the safest place, e.g.
   (a) Out of draughts from windows and doors.
   (b) Not in a corner.
   (c) Never near a door — danger when oven door is opened.
2. Pan guards should be fitted where there are small children.
3. Oven cloths and matches must not be left on cooker.
4. A thick oven cloth or gloves should be used to take dishes out of the oven.
5. Wipe grease spills up at once.
6. Frying: (a) Pan not more than half full.
              (b) Safer not to have boiling kettle near fat pan.
              (c) Don't leave extra oil or fat on or near cooker.
7. Turn pan handles away from edge of cooker but not over burners or hot plates.

Surfaces and materials

1. Non-slip, even floor coverings. Wipe up spills at once.
2. Plenty of work tops.
3. Non-flammable curtains or none at all if cooker is near window.

Knives

1. Must be sharp — safer for working than blunt ones.
2. Don't leave them near the edge of the table.
3. Wash and put away when finished with.
4. Carry at side, point downwards.

Cleaning liquids etc.

1. Keep out of children's reach — the under-sink cupboard is only safe if it locks.
2. Never put them in lemonade bottles etc.
3. Don't keep them in the larder.
4. Keep labels clean (pour from opposite side).
5. Use as directed — don't breathe in fumes.

Lighting and ventilation

1. Must be able to see properly whenever work is being done, e.g. may need extra lights over cooker, work tops or sink.

2. Need good ventilation — bad ventilation induces fatigue which causes accidents. Try to avoid draughts.
3. Extraction fans, cooker hoods should be used if possible.

Fires

1. Put in safest place — wall mounted often best.
2. Properly guarded.
3. Properly installed and regularly checked.

Water

1. Temperature of hot water should not be above 60°C for ordinary working purposes.
2. Take extra care that boilers (especially small ones on cookers) don't boil over.
3. Keep lid on copper, washing machine, etc. even if water is not hot — small children can tumble in and be drowned.
4. Don't put electric kettles on floor to boil.
5. Keep dishes of hot liquid away from edge of table etc.

Work clothes

1. Loose clothes, apron strings catch on door handles, equipment etc.
2. Well-fastened, low-heeled shoes in good condition safest.
3. Non-inflammable aprons worth making.

General

1. Small step-ladder safer for reaching high places.
2. All equipment placed for safety, e.g. shelves not too high, heavy articles put on lower shelves.
3. Tidy working very important.
4. Some first aid equipment should be handy (apart from the main first aid box in the house).
5. Some fire fighting appliance should be in, or near, kitchen, e.g. blanket, sand, soil etc.
6. Children — if possible working area should be fenced off so that they can't get near dangerous equipment (especially when at crawling or toddling stage).
7. Pets — safest kept out of kitchen — it helps if you feed them somewhere else.
8. Put plastic bags away safely at once if there are small children.

Definitions

Au gratin. A dish coated with sauce, sprinkled with breadcrumbs or cheese (or both) and browned under the grill or in the oven.

Bake blind. Pastry cases baked without a filling.

Baste. Spooning hot fat or other liquid over food during cooking, to keep it moist.

Blanch. Cover food with cold water, bring to boil, strain, rinse — cold water. Useful for:
(*a*) Removing skins from nuts and tomatoes.
(*b*) To whiten bones, meat, etc.
(*c*) To remove strong flavour.

Blend. To mix smoothly, usually a starchy powder plus a liquid.

Bouquet garni. A small bunch of herbs tied together and used to flavour soups and stews, e.g. parsley, thyme, marjoram and bay leaf. Remove before serving.

Canapé. Fingers or shapes of bread (plain, fried or toasted) or pastry, used as a base for savouries or hors d'oeuvres.

Croûtons. Bread cut into small dice or fancy shapes, then fried. Served with purée soups and some savoury dishes.

Enzymes. Chemical substances which cause chemical changes to take place, such as the breakdown of food during digestion, fruit to ripen. Enzymes are found in the human body, yeast, fruits etc.

Forcemeat. Stuffing — e.g. sage and onion.

Food. Any solid or liquid swallowed which provides the body with nutrients.
Note: Roughage and pepper are not nutrients.

Fricasseé. A white stew of chicken, veal or rabbit.

Garnish. A decoration for savoury dishes to add colour and flavour and improve the appearance, e.g. parsley, sliced tomato, etc.

Glaze. To give food a glossy surface, e.g. pies, buns, scones, flans.
Some glazes — egg, milk, sugar and water, thickened fruit juice.

Hors d'oeuvres. Small portions of appetising savoury food.
Served at the beginning of dinner or lunch. Usually served cold.
Foods suitable: Melon, grapefruit, varieties of salad foods, meat, fish, eggs.

Liaison. Thickening or binding used for soups and sauces, e.g. flour, egg yolk, cream.

Macedoine. A mixture of vegetables or of fruit, cut into dice.

Malnutrition. Occurs when the body doesn't get the right amount or the right proportion of the nutrients. A person can get 'plenty to eat' and still suffer from malnutrition.

Panada. A thick sauce used to bind ingredients together, e.g. for croquettes, vegetarian cutlets, etc.

Parboil. To partly cook by boiling and then to finish cooking by another method — e.g. potatoes parboiled then roasted.

Pulses. Dried peas, beans and lentils.

Purée. The smooth pulp obtained by pressing food through a sieve, usually vegetables or fruit, sometimes fish or meat.

Soups made with sieved ingredients are called purée soups.

Raspings. Scraps of stale bread slowly dried and browned in the oven, then crushed with a rolling pin and sieved.

Used to coat fish, etc. before frying.

Réchauffé. Left-over food re-heated, or made into a new dish and re-heated.

Roux. Fat and flour cooked together (usually in equal quantities).

Used to thicken sauces, soups, stews.

Sauté. To cook food by tossing it in a little hot fat, e.g. sauté potatoes.

Vol-au-vent. A large puff pastry case. (Small ones are called bouchées.)

The cases may be filled with savoury or sweet fillings.

Zest. The outside skin of citrus fruits. It contains the oil which gives the flavour. It must be peeled off very thinly so that there is no white pith on it.

Oven temperatures

The numbering of oven temperatures varies with different cookers. The following is a general guide.

	Electric (Degrees Fahrenheit)	Gas
Very slow	250–275	$\frac{1}{2}$–1
Slow	300–325	2–3
Moderate	350	4
Moderately hot	375	5
Hot	400–425	6–7
Very hot	450–500	8–9

Some temperature equivalents (rounded off to the nearest 10°C).

F	C
250	130
300	150
350	180
375	190
400	200
425	220
450	230
500	260